To The Mulgrews –
Have a merrily
independent Christmas!
Love from
Gerda

Unstated

Writers on Scottish Independence

and

Cyrus

Edited by Scott Hames

...ember 2012

WP BOOKS

Published by Word Power Books 2012
43–45 West Nicolson Street
Edinburgh EH8 9DB
www.word-power.co.uk

Printed and bound by Martins the Printers, Berwick upon Tweed.
Designed by Leela Sooben

British Library Cataloguing in Publication Data.
A catalogue record for this book is available from the British Library.
ISBN 978-0-9566283-9-8

Any proceeds due to the editor will be donated
to the Scottish Refugee Council.

The publisher acknowledges support from Creative Scotland
towards the publication of this title.

CREATIVE SCOTLAND

ALBA | CHRUTHACHAIL

CONTENTS

Introduction   1
John Aberdein   19
Allan Armstrong   25
Alan Bissett   32
Jenni Calder   39
Bob Cant   46
Jo Clifford   52
Meaghan Delahunt   57
Douglas Dunn   62
Margaret Elphinstone   71
Leigh French and Gordon Asher   77
Janice Galloway   88
Magi Gibson   95
Alasdair Gray   100
Kirsty Gunn   111
Kathleen Jamie   115
James Kelman   118
Tom Leonard   126

Ken MacLeod   128
Aonghas MacNeacail   133
Kevin MacNeil   140
Denise Mina   149
Don Paterson   156
James Robertson   165
Suhayl Saadi   172
Mike Small   179
Gerda Stevenson   186
Christopher Whyte   193
Notes on Contributors   199

INTRODUCTION

Don't Feel Bought, You're Buying

Weeks before the 1979 referendum on devolution, William McIlvanney sensed a mood of national stock-taking. 'Faced with the strangeness of where we had come to, we were perhaps more inclined to wonder about the strangeness of how we had got there.'[1] A similar feeling is with us now. The Free Presbyterian Kirk has just warned that Scottish statehood 'would be a provocation of God'.[2] Perhaps this is what Rupert Murdoch meant by arguing Scotland should be allowed to take its own risks.[3]

Part of the current strangeness is the murky place of 'culture' in the political shift implied by the upcoming referendum on independence. The very phrase would have sounded miraculous to cultural nationalists in March 1979, when McIlvanney lambasted 'The Cowardly Lion' who chose the feeding bowl over 'the terrible distances of freedom'. But how much distance really has been run since then, and what role have writers and artists played in crossing it?

In the years following the 1979 debacle, it is commonly argued, Scotland achieved 'a form of cultural autonomy in the absence of its political equivalent', led above all by novelists, poets and dramatists.[4] Writers such as Alasdair Gray, Tom Leonard, James Kelman and Liz Lochhead are held to have energised a wider cultural debate concerning national identity and self-determination, and to have exercised a quasi-democratic function in the period leading up to, and in some sense preparing the ground for, devolution. In 1998 Christopher Whyte argued that 'in the absence of elected political authority, the task of representing the nation has been repeatedly devolved to its writers'.[5] So effective were Scottish writers in this symbolic role, when the new parliament finally opened Liam McIlvanney was struck by 'how little it now seemed to matter'.

> Its coming was welcome, certainly, but hardly seemed critical to the nation's cultural health. Above all, it was belated: by the time the Parliament arrived, a revival in Scottish fiction had been long underway ... Without waiting for the politicians, Scottish novelists had written themselves out of despair.[6]

The shift from despondency to assurance in one generation of McIlvanneys is striking, but the notion of Scottish culture as a political surrogate has a longer history. 'The overwhelming tenor of Scottish nationalism was cultural rather than political', write Christopher Harvie and Peter Jones; referring not to the age of 7:84 and Runrig but that of Stevenson, Barrie and Patrick Geddes.[7] If the impulse toward asserting Scottish identity in the 1880-90s 'hinged on the grievances of a successful but subordinate imperial partner that its distinctiveness was not sufficiently recognised', today's cultural politics of Scottish emancipation are something like the reverse, defined against the ethic of imperial/Anglo-American partnership and, after the *Braveheart* comedown, dissatisfied by atavistic sops to 'identity'. Or so it seems: Alex Salmond spent part of the summer promoting a cod-feminist cartoon about 'lovable indigenous aristocrats', in James Kelman's description.[8] (According to the chair of VisitScotland, Disney-Pixar's movie 'is about changing your fate and I believe it will change the fate of Scottish tourism in a significant and positive way'.[9] Could there be a more servile gloss on a film entitled *Brave*?)

It wasn't fate that a nationalist government should find itself reducing Scottish culture to tourist-bait, and the arts to 'creative industries'. In other places culture is the motor of nationalism, not the hood ornament. Murray Pittock points out that 'the shift to culturalism after political defeat had been the road taken in Ireland for twenty years following the fall of Parnell in 1891'. To the extent this path was trodden in Scotland after 1979, it seldom – despite appearances – intersected with organised political nationalism. The modern SNP, Pittock reminds us, 'was frequently almost indifferent to cultural matters', and set little store by arguments for linguistic renaissance or artistic heritage.[10] Unlike comparable nationalist parties in Catalonia or Quebec, 'the types of issue the SNP mobilised around from its inception revolved around self-government/independence in addition to a range of social and economic issues … Significantly, such mobilisations seldom involved language or cultural issues'.[11]

At times the indifference was mutual. Jack Brand spent an entire chapter of his 1978 study of *The National Movement in Scotland* contrasting literary nationalism of the inter-war period – 'for the poets and other writers of [the 1920s and 30s] nationalism was a key issue: even *the* key issue' – with the post-50s scene in which the lions of Rose Street had become an unofficial establishment with few obvious heirs. What political enthusiasm had survived into the 1960s found an outlet in New Left commitment, and for younger writers, wrote Brand on the eve of the first referendum, 'the concern with Scotland as a nation is hardly discernible. Most of them have written about persons or situations which were identifiably Scottish but this did not have the implication of being concerned with the political issue'.[12] Only Norman MacCaig and Nigel Tranter feature, peripherally, as literary figures directly involved in the 1979 campaigns (as members of the 'Yes for Scotland' committee), not forgetting the more diffuse but undoubtedly potent influence of Home Rulers such as Hamish Henderson.[13] Today a few prominent writers are, with varying degrees of wariness, taking the plunge and aligning themselves overtly with the official campaigns, while others signal their enthusiasm or scepticism – and often both – from a distance.

In 1977 Tom Nairn traced Scotland's long, oblique tradition of *cultural sub-nationalism* within the Union:

> Cultural, because of course it could not be political; on the other hand this culture could not be straightforwardly nationalist either – a direct substitute for political action … It could only be 'sub-nationalist', in the sense of venting its national content in various crooked ways – neurotically, so to speak, rather than directly.[14]

Throughout the nineteenth century, Nairn showed, Scotland's deep reservoir of shallow display-identities remained largely untapped, 'latent and unexploited' as a vehicle for conventional cultural nationalism.[15] But in the 1960s, 'once the material circumstances for a new sort of political mobilisation had formed', the sturdy icons of Scottish sub-culture – however 'deformed', and despite the 'inexpressible pain' they cause intellectuals – were ready and waiting: 'the thistle patch proved very useful'.[16] The SNP were able to capitalise on the currency and emotional salience of Scottish difference, without committing to a culturalist politics of 'tradition' and revival.

After 1979 it becomes difficult to separate the politicisation of Scottish culture (that is, the electoral mobilisation of sub-nationalism) from the *culturalisation* of Scottish politics. The general election results of the 1980s made the reality of a distinct Scottish polity – one consistently voting for governments it did not get – a question not only of democratic representation but national affirmation. The 'expression of political difference' achieved by Scottish votes against Thatcher / Major, David McCrone observed in 1992, 'has developed without the encumbrance of heavy cultural baggage', and seemed not to manifest a 'specific *cultural* divergence'.[17] If the divergence of Scottish politics had little 'cultural' content, it undoubtedly had cultural consequences. In 1993 Neal Ascherson observed that '"Scottishness" used to be a private thing. Now, under the stagnant surface, it is being steadily politicised. It has come to include the sense of being governed against one's will by the preferences of another, larger nation'.[18] The slow-motion legitimation crisis by which Tory support limped toward the Doomsday Scenario gleefully forecast by *Radical Scotland* in 1987 – the election of a Conservative government with no Scottish mandate whatsoever[19] – encouraged the 'general elision between political and cultural representation' in Scotland. Noting this pattern in 1992, Pat Kane saw a role for Scottishness beyond that of badge or thistle-patch. 'Cultural autonomy has been a crucial substratum for political autonomy', and could be so again, but actively and on terms shaped by artists rather than politicians.[20] And yet artists do not choose the ideological climate in which their work is received. James Kelman's defiant acceptance speech of the 1994 Booker Prize – 'my culture and my language have the right to exist, and no one has the authority to dismiss that' – was misread as a nationalist *cri-de-coeur*. (The first question he was asked in the press conference afterward: 'why do you hate the English so much?') For the past twenty years, it has been very difficult to locate the politics of individual Scottish writers (or their artworks) in any context separable from politicised national identity – a pattern sponsoring the reduction of all politics to identity politics.

More route than destination

And today? Two of the histories cited above are called *The Road to Home Rule* and *The Road to Independence?* We are running out of road, and approaching a major junction. But the object of all this heady momentum, frequently disparaged as a mere 'vehicle', remains mysterious. Would the SNP's sort of independence be a platform for wider social transformation, or a self-serving end in itself? In 1979, McIlvanney described the SNP as 'more route than destination'; in 1989 Nairn expressed his fear that SNP-ism amounted to a ring-road of deliverance, in which the self-appointed party of destiny was perpetually enacting liberation simply by remaining in power.[21] A qualified distrust of the SNP remains strong among the writers I've contacted in the course of assembling this book.

And on the other side? At the launch of the 'No' campaign Alistair Darling warned against 'going on a journey with an uncertain destination'. But if the destination is known in advance, it is not a journey at all. If going nowhere is the essential message of 'Better Together', it could do worse than to hop aboard the Inverness bus-route noted in John Aberdein's essay. 'Culloden via Tesco' has a suggestive bathos as we approach an historic crucible by way of retail politics. *Buy autonomy get equality half-price. Premium defence contracts while supplies – and the Union – last.* This cheapness found its cultural level at the 'No' launch when pro-Union celebrity Miss Inverness 2010 let it be known that 'there is nothing I like better than donning my tartan mini-skirt'.[22] Emphasis on the *sub*-nationalism, then. Are we really back to the thistle patch, and has any distance been covered at all since the 1970s?

Were Scottish cultural figures really in the driving-seat of devolution, or were they just impressive passengers, adorning a process fuelled by concerns quite different to their own? Holyrood has its Makardom and the Canongate Wall, honouring the symbolic role played by Scottish writers in bringing the parliament into being, but the selfsame writers seem largely ornamental in the current debate, politely revered when wheeled-on as ciphers of Scottishness but whose views are not expected to set the agenda. It is difficult to imagine a writer of McIlvanney's moral seriousness being invited to address a major party's annual conference today, as the SNP did in 1987. (McIlvanney took the opportunity to dub Mrs Thatcher a 'cultural vandal', strengthening the notion that Thatcherism was fundamentally at odds with Scottish communitarian traditions.) His shift in alignment from Labour to SNP in 1996 was a front-page splash;[23] by contrast the National Makar's speech at the official launch of the 'Yes' campaign was barely covered by media more interested in the endorsements of Hollywood actors.[24]

Recalling the strangeness of Scotland's organised political nationalism, decried by Nairn as 'an apolitical and anti-cultural nationalism unique in the world', it might be fairest to say that 'culture' contributed a great deal to the formation and recognition of a mobilisable Scottish identity, but the electoral beneficiaries of that mobilisation had little firm interest in culture as an end in itself. Their actions in office bear this out, and here history repeats itself. In that infamous year of civic boosterism, Glasgow's 1990, Angus Calder questioned the cash-value of Scottish left-wing culturalism:

> Even if you throw in a few anti-apartheid songs and musical contributions from Chile and Nicaragua, what have the *uses* of popular culture which have been *made* by the labour movement in Scotland helped to achieve? Total Labour Party dominance in Lowland Scotland voting patterns and the yuppification of central Glasgow and the Old Town of Edinburgh, that's what, if anything, they have helped to achieve.[25]

This is a valuable reminder. Writers, musicians and performers may have articulated a sense of Scottish disenfranchisement in the 1980s and 90s, and brought the 'substratum' of cultural autonomy to the electoral surface. But the conservative political process we call 'devolution' – no more or less than an effort to re-legitimise the UK state – was, in the end, not meaningfully shaped by them. To read some cultural histories of the past few decades, you would think Holyrood was dreamed into being by artists. It wasn't. That the name of 'Alisdair Gray' is misspelled on the Canongate Wall is fitting, and installs a necessary distance between the cultural and political processes at issue. Make no mistake: the Scotland Act was the outcome of decades' worth of short-term electoral venality by the major UK parties, realised only via anti-democratic machine politics of sometimes breath-taking cynicism.[26]

The one writer who is making an impact on the current debate is doing so via his estate, rather than his art. On his death in 2010 Edwin Morgan bequested nearly a million pounds to the SNP, which the party ring-fenced for a referendum campaign following its victory in the 2011 Holyrood elections. This direct alignment between literature and nationalism makes it all the more important to attend to the ambivalence of what Morgan actually wrote. In 1991 he penned 'A Warning' to jubilant ex-citizens of the Soviet Union, fearing that liberation might amount to no more than a retro-fitting of what came before, and the resurrection of forces 'that never will grow freedom'.

Musty but indefatigable reaction
stirs half-incredulously on one elbow
in another tomb as the bells clang, whistles,
laughs, clacks his grubby bones and orders suitings,
modest, subfusc, meeting the *novus ordo*
with decency. What, a republic a kingdom?
No no, there's nothing waiting in the wings, it's
early days. Take your string bag. An orange
will appear by magic, steaks, heroin, tickets
for strippers. Don't feel bought, you're buying, buying.
— And if, oh, if any should stint the euphoria
for a moment, watching the snow falling softly
over shot-pocked facades, there'd only be some
muffled echo of the better life that
never seems to come, like a faint singing
heard in the pauses of snoring out of cardboard
or waiters' shouts from bursting blood-red kitchens.
They must listen so very hard, the freed ones![27]

Post-communist caution gains another resonance in Scotland today. Seeing huge crowds celebrate the collapse of the Soviet empire, Morgan 'felt like warning them through the television set – do you really know what you've done ... do you really know what problems lie ahead for you? I felt this very strongly just because I had hoped so much when I was young, I suppose'.[28] It would be absurd to map this scenario directly onto the current state of Scottish culture and politics, but both the hope and the warning seem pertinent as the referendum on independence draws near. We should listen very hard to what is being muffled and suppressed in the clamorous debate over Scotland's future. Despite his direct posthumous contribution to the fortunes of political nationalism, Morgan himself was neither buying nor bought when it came to cut-price visions of liberation, nor doom-mongering about its economic cost. The relevance of his poem to our present circumstances, to be clear, is not its note of ca' canny hesitation in the face of dramatic change, but its warning not to mistake the true nature of the choices and freedoms in prospect.

Even at this early stage of the referendum campaign, we are deluged by facile arguments and factoids designed to 'manage' debate, or to rig the terrain on which it is contested. As the politicians sharpen their messaging and reduce the discussion to slogans, fantasies and nightmares, it is increasingly apparent that the truly thorny, exciting and difficult questions about self-determination – including the basis of that national 'self' – will be submerged and hidden from view. Before the party machines and newspapers settle the parameters of a bogus debate, there must be room for more radical, more honest and more nuanced thinking about what 'independence' means in and for Scottish culture. The aims of this collection are two-fold. First, to set the question of Scottish political independence within the much wider and often radical horizons which inform these writers' work, both as artists and public intellectuals. Second, to document the true relationship between the official discourse of Scottish nationalism, and the ethical concerns of some of the writers presented as its guiding lights and cultural guarantors.

The political significance of these writers' work is also at stake in the deepening of the conflation that equates Scottish identity with nationalism. 'If Scotland voted for *political* devolution in 1997', argues Cairns Craig,

> it had much earlier declared *cultural* devolution, both in the radical voices of new Scottish writing – from James Kelman to Matthew Fitt, from Janice Galloway to Ali Smith – and in the rewriting of Scottish cultural history that produced, in the 1980s and 1990s, a new sense of the richness and the autonomy of Scotland's past cultural achievements.[29]

It sometimes sounds as though the dissenting energies of post-1979 Scottish literary culture can only find political realisation when subsumed within the discourse of liberal nationalism. Such readings risk the silent appropriation of more radical currents in the writing at issue, re-channeling them toward debates which exclude in advance any alternative to neoliberal capitalism and parliamentary democracy. More politically adventurous and provocative moments in recent Scottish writing – moments unmistakably rejecting this neutered political vision – are quietly omitted from this uplifting story, in which the political relevance of Scottish literature is delimited in advance to the affirmation and recuperation of 'identity'.

This project emerges from a conviction that the relationship between contemporary Scottish literature and contemporary Scottish politics is much more ambivalent, charged and complex than this critical narrative would suggest. The politics of Scottish devolution, and the contemporary debate over political independence, are self-evidently far less radical, passionate and imaginative than the politics of the writers most often invoked as symbols of their 'cultural' rootedness and legitimacy.

Independence from the independence debate

The idea for this book assumed that prominent Scottish writers would feature in the rhetoric of both official campaigns, but also that the views of individual writers would be managed, 'storied', inflated and filtered in various distorting ways. It's early days, but it seems the views of writers may not be sufficiently influential to warrant such interference. It was, however, front-page news when 'Nobel Laureate Mario Vargas Llosa warned independence could produce a provincial vision of the world's social and political problems and claimed it would be sad if it goes ahead'.[30] This statement prompted a vigorous series of letters arguing for and against Llosa's rather vague impression of Scottish nationalism as 'tribal', but – curiously to me – none of the letter-writers countered or even contextualised a story headlined 'Writer blasts nationalists' by referring to the known views of *Scottish* writers. (The conspiratorially minded will have noticed that these stories omitted to mention Llosa's own political alignment with 'Andean Thatcherism'.)

Perhaps it is better to be ignored than to be manipulated. A week after the announcement of McIlvanney's SNP 'conversion' in 1996, he documented the embellishment and exploitation of his response to a journalist's question.

> I find offensive the extent to which this basic message ['I have no alienation now to the thought of voting SNP'] has been distorted into whatever people who seem to think only in sound-bites want it to mean. It seems almost impossible in the petrified forest of party politics here to make a statement that doesn't harden instantly into being merely part of a moribund set of preconceptions. Anything you say will be misconstrued and used in evidence against you at the drumhead court of mindless party dogma. I think I have had enough of this.[31]

Small wonder that later writers have steered clear of party-political entanglement. Both out of curiosity and in the interest of posterity, I wanted to circumvent such worries and record what various Scottish writers really thought about the independence question, in a context free from the noise and enforced concision of the media debate. A second motivation was to construct a space in which the questions, priorities and histories likely to be studiously avoided in the official campaigns could be properly explored by Scottish writers and activists with something to say. This book attempts to stand back from both official campaigns on the independence question – indeed, to win a degree of independence from them – and to set the choices before us within parameters chosen by writers themselves.

What of the choice of writers for this book? This is no attempt to constitute a pantheon of 'authors whose voices must be heard' – plenty of writers not in this book should be and are being heard. Neither was there any particular attempt to be 'representative' (canonically, sociologically, politically), or to achieve a 'balance' of opinions and identities. Because academics and journalists are finding their own ways into the 'official' debate, we've focused on novelists, poets, playwrights, editors and translators. There is an unembarrassed bias towards people actively engaged in the politics of Scottish culture. Fewer than half the writers who accepted our invitation and sent us an essay are women (10 of 27). About two-thirds of the male writers we invited, accepted; for women it was about half. The collection is very, even uncomfortably white, but then so is the culture it's talking about.

Early days?

Morgan's 'nothing waiting in the wings, it's / early days' cannot but recall the unofficial credo of Scottish cultural nationalism, Alasdair Gray's 'work as if you were living in the early days of a better nation'. Those imagined early days have a history all their own. As Gray has grown tired of acknowledging, this resonant phrase derives from the Canadian poet Dennis Lee. Considerably less sunny than Gray's slogan, Lee's long 1972 poem *Civil Elegies* is no encomium to nation-building, but a tormented meditation on voided citizenship. Far from the promise of a clean slate, the poem dwells on national defeat, 'honour[ing] each one of my country's failures of nerve and its sellouts'.[32] But even knowledge of its own abnegation is worthless 'in a nation of / losers and quislings' content 'to fashion / other men's napalm and know it'.[33] (Officially, Canada abstained from the US war on Vietnam.)

Gray's is the more attractive vision, but Lee's poem is a reminder that it is entirely possible to remain dominated, and complicit, from behind your own 'sovereign' borders. If that was true four decades ago, it is all the more so today. 'The trajectory of even the most heroic nationalist movement', Alex Callinicos argues, 'is to carve out its own space within the capitalist world system and therefore ultimately make its peace with that system'.[34] This is a criticism from the radical left, but comes suggestively close to the SNP's rhetoric of 'normalisation'.

A year before Lee's poem was published in its final form, the Edinburgh poet Alan Jackson argued that the individual freedom of the writer was partly at stake in the debates of a renascent Scottish literary nationalism. With a tang of hippy individualism, Jackson argued that the price of the liberation promised by nationalism was 'continu[ing] the myths by which a few can act on behalf of many'.

Are we too to have *our* frontiers and passports, our *own* call-up papers and definition of undesirable aliens? A new form of loyalty and so a new form of surrender?[35]

To put Jackson's reminder another way, the fulfilment of nationalist desire lies not in 'un-neurotic' cultural Scottishness, but political statehood, including its unlovely apparatus. (Look closely at Chad McCail's cover.) Others will insist the status quo can hardly be preferable, when the broken democratic machinery of the UK guarantees rule by a 'few' elected by a different 'many', depriving Scotland of responsibility as well as agency.

Many would argue that new forms of artistic loyalty and surrender are being enforced already. If devolution is the child of Scottish cultural radicalism, a terrible revenge has been visited on the parent. In 2003 Cairns Craig presciently noted 'the threat of a culture of compliance' as Scottish Executive strategic plans fully integrated arts policy with wider government aims, nowhere acknowledging the good and necessary function 'of *critique*, of *opposition*, of *refusal*, of *challenge* … The arts, it seems, produce only harmony and inclusiveness'. The Scottish Arts Council of the 1970s and 80s, wrote Craig,

> found itself playing a disruptive role in the British body politic and assisting in a flourishing culture of resistance to the established political structure. The question is whether such a Scottish culture can survive the managerial harmonisation of its purposes *within* government policy.[36]

By a grim irony, the cultural sector held to blaze the trail for Scottish political autonomy now finds itself dominated by home-grown governmentality, valued chiefly as an economic resource, a lever of public policy, and as a 'service' to be effectively and efficiently delivered. Craig makes his disgust plain in noting that the 'National Cultural Strategy' for 2002-2007 envisions literature solely as 'a means to the fulfilment of the general government policy of making Scotland fit for globalised capitalism'.[37] As this book goes to press a number of writers involved in it have united to protest the vision of 'culture' evident in the conduct and remit of Creative Scotland.[38]

There is a rich history of critical debate concerning the relationship between Scottish culture and Scottish nationalism. This is only a brief sketch of some of the positions and narratives which have informed the debate over the past few decades. Writers unable to align their nationality with an existing state – the un-stated – will, I am sure, be keeping all these questions on the table. Let it remain their table. The passions, queries and visions of the essays collected in this book seem likely to remain largely 'outside' the official discourse on independence, but here they are, stated in their own space.

Scott Hames
Stirling, November 2012

A note on timing

This book was assembled in the spring and summer of 2012, with the majority of essays submitted between May and July. Needless to say, the referendum debate has not stood still during this time, and developments after August 2012 are not reflected or rebutted.

A note on texts

Douglas Dunn's poem appeared previously in *New Poems, Chiefly in the Scottish Dialect*, ed. Robert Crawford (Polygon, 2009); Janice Galloway's essay expands on a piece written for the *Guardian* in August 2011; James Kelman's essay first appeared in *NY Arts* magazine; Tom Leonard's second image previously appeared in his collection *outside the narrative* (Etruscan/Word Power, 2009). Our thanks to Edwin Morgan's Literary Executors, and to Carcanet, for permission to cite Morgan's poem 'A Warning'.

NOTES

[1]   William McIlvanney, 'Before: February 1979 – Referendum' in *Surviving the Shipwreck* (Edinburgh: Mainstream, 1991), pp. 17-22 (p. 18).

[2]   Alasdair Munro, 'Scottish independence: Self rule would be a "provocation of God" say Wee Frees', *Scotsman*, 19 June 2012.

[3]   On 20 February 2012, Murdoch tweeted 'Let Scotland go and compete. Everyone would win'. This followed a message declaring Alex Salmond 'clearly most brilliant politician in UK'. Simon Johnson, 'Rupert Murdoch takes to Twitter to back Scottish independence', *Telegraph*, 21 February 2012.

[4]   Murray Pittock, *The Road to Independence?* (London: Reaktion, 2008), p. 114. See also Pittock, pp. 114-35; Michael Gardiner, *Modern Scottish Culture* (Edinburgh: Edinburgh University Press, 2005), pp. 144-61. For a deft critique of this narrative see Alex Thomson, '"You can't get there from here": Devolution and Scottish literary history', *International Journal of Scottish Literature* 3 (2007) [www.ijsl.stir.ac.uk].

[5]   Christopher Whyte, 'Masculinities in Contemporary Scottish Fiction', *Forum for Modern Language Studies* 34.2 (1998), 274-85 (p. 284).

[6]   Liam McIlvanney, 'The Politics of Narrative in the Post-War Scottish Novel' in *On Modern British Fiction*, ed. Zachary Leader (Oxford: Oxford University Press, 2002), pp. 181-208 (p. 183).

[7]   Christopher Harvie and Peter Jones, *The Road to Home Rule* (Edinburgh: Polygon, 2000), p. 25.

[8]   James Kelman, 'The British Council and the Edinburgh Writers Conference', 13 August 2012 [www.word-power.co.uk].

[9]   'Alex Salmond attending US premier of Disney film Brave', BBC News online, 18 June 2012 [www.bbc.co.uk/news/uk-scotland-scotland-business-18467968].

[10]   *The Road to Independence?*, p. 114.

[11]   Peter Lynch, 'The Scottish National Party: The Long Road from Marginality to Blackmail and Coalition Potential' in *Autonomist Parties in Europe: Identity Politics and the Revival of the Territorial Cleavage, Vol I.*, ed. by Lieven De Winter et al (Barcelona: Institut de Ciències Polítiques i Socials, 2006), pp. 227–51 (p. 231).

[12]   Jack Brand, *The National Movement In Scotland* (London: Routledge, 1978), p. 90.

[13]   Allan Macartney, 'The Protagonists' in *The Referendum Experience: Scotland 1979*

ed. by John Bochel, David Denver and Allan Macartney (Aberdeen: Aberdeen University Press, 1981), pp. 12-42 (p. 26).

[14] Tom Nairn, *The Break-Up of Britain* 2nd edn (London: Verso, 1981), p. 156.

[15] Ibid, pp. 141-2.

[16] Ibid, p. 131.

[17] David McCrone, *Understanding Scotland: The Sociology of a Stateless Nation* (London: Routledge, 1992), pp. 195-6.

[18] Neal Ascherson, 'The warnings that Scotland's patient nationalism could turn nasty', *Independent*, 21 November 1993.

[19] See *Radical Scotland* 25, Feb/March 1987.

[20] Pat Kane, 'Artistic Rage That Cultivates the Scottish Consensus', *Guardian*, 6 February 1992.

[21] Tom Nairn, 'The Timeless Girn' in *A Claim of Right for Scotland*, ed. by Owen Dudley Edwards (Edinburgh: Polygon, 1989), pp. 163-78.

[22] Magnus Gardham, 'United for Scotland; Labour, Tories and Lib Dems Say We're Better Together', *Daily Record*, 26 June 2012.

[23] Robin Dinwoodie, 'New chapter as McIlvanney endorses nationalists', *Herald*, 6 April 1996.

[24] Brian Currie, 'A-listers and well-wishers line up for independence', *Herald*, 26 May 2012; Severin Carrell, 'Alex Salmond predicts million-strong movement for Scottish independence', *Guardian* online, 25 May 2012 [www.guardian.co.uk/politics/2012/may/25/alex-salmond-yes-scotland-independence]. It should be noted that Liz Lochhead spoke in a personal capacity.

[25] Angus Calder, 'Worker's Culture – Popular Culture – Defining Our Terms' in *Revolving Culture: Notes from the Scottish Republic* [1990] (London: I.B. Tauris, 1994), pp. 229-242 (p. 232).

[26] See, among other sources, Vernon Bogdanor, *Devolution in the United Kingdom* (Oxford: Oxford University Press, 2001), pp. 110-143, 166-200; T.M. Devine, *The Scottish Nation 1700-2000* (London: Penguin, 1999), pp. 574-590; James Kellas, 'On To An Assembly?' in *The Referendum Experience: Scotland 1979* ed. by John Bochel, David Denver and Allan Macartney (Aberdeen: Aberdeen University Press, 1981), pp. 147-52; Graham Walker, 'The "Scotland is British" Campaign, 1976-8' in *Scottish Affairs* 61 (2009): 74-100.

[27] *Sweeping Out The Dark* (Manchester: Carcanet, 1994). First published in *Hold Hands Among the Atoms* (Edinburgh: Mariscat, 1991).

[28] Unpublished interview, quoted by Colin Nicholson in *Edwin Morgan: Inventions of Modernity* (Manchester: Manchester University Press, 2002), pp. 157-8.

[29] Cairns Craig, 'Scotland: Culture After Devolution' in *Ireland (Ulster) Scotland: Concepts, Contexts, Comparisons*, ed. Edna Longley, Eamonn Hughes and Des O'Rawe (Belfast: Cló Ollscoil na Banríona, 2003), pp. 39-49 (p. 39).

[30] Victoria Weldon, 'Writer blasts nationalists', *Herald*, 9 June 2012.

[31] William McIlvanney, 'Country Before Party', *Herald*, 13 April 1996.

[32] Dennis Lee, *Civil Elegies and Other Poems* (Toronto: Anansi, 1972), p. 55.

[33] Ibid., pp. 44, 48.

[34] Alex Callinicos, 'Marxism and the National Question' in *Scotland, Class and Nation*, ed. Chris Bambery (London: Bookmarks, 1999), pp. 37-50 (p. 47).

[35] Alan Jackson, 'The Knitted Claymore', *Lines Review* 37 (1971): 2-38 (p. 8).

[36] Craig, 'Scotland: Culture After Devolution', p. 43.

[37] Ibid, p. 42.

[38] Don Paterson's essay for this volume was published online by *The Herald* on 14 September 2012. In the weeks following, the Scottish arts community applied significant pressure to the management and ideology of Creative Scotland, to what effect remains to be seen.

JOHN ABERDEIN

I have contracted an aversion to *hype*. It is a bog-standard Rannoch Moor aversion, neither world class nor premier league. And so, if the Electoral Commission sanctions the extra box, I might not vote in the referendum *Yes* – but merely *Uhuh*. Imagine, if you will, a tottering pile of *Uhuhs*. Because we have had a measure of independence for quite some time – but what have we done with it?

We have had powers over primary and secondary education for donkeys' years, yet our education system is confounded by hype. *Quality Assurance, Higher Still,* and now *Curriculum for Excellence.* Cream is not enough for the mandarins: they must churn the schools till they get butter. The perfectability of children – or the system – lies within our grasp, it is implied, just a couple of documents off. I enjoyed teaching in Scotland for nearly thirty years, but to re-enter the classroom under such pressures would do my nut. We don't need independence to sort this: we need to let a whole variety of teachers with high commitment – and proper pay and pensions – proceed with the professional confidence that accords and comes with democratic power. See the Kirkland Five. See Finland.

Similarly, we have had serious devolution for a while now, with control over our National Health Service, yet much of our individual health is raddled. We gollop fast food down, we drink like whales. Pigging and whaling it because we are not independent? Perhaps with independence – and Trident gone – we could create a new defence policy, winching our more gaseous bodies up as barrage balloons. Creative Scotland likes big projects. Otherwise, with respect to egalitarian models of individual health targeting and collective improvement, again see Finland.

And we have had a Scottish Parliament for thirteen years, re-engaged to a proud old legal system, with control over our country's infinitely toured, dearly cherished land – yet we barely know who owns the bugger, except it isn't us. There is a fault that lies across our land, but it is our fault, not Westminster's. That gaping fault comprises: land theft from the commons; land left waste and underused; land exclusion still unrighted. Read the Landman: Andy Wightman.

So there is national and local hype, but a general miasma. *Aberdeen*, it says on an airport billboard as you enter the terminal: *home of the self-sealing envelope*. There's no answer to that. A worser silence hangs about *Dounreay, home of weapons-grade plutonium*. And as we seek to found a planet-saving, high-export, steel-hungry, renewables industry, we meet the sign – *Ravenscraig, home of globalism (flitted)*. Scotia, home of hames, hame of homes, can aye domesticate apocalypse.

There was a day in my youth when you could walk dryshod across the Atlantic from Ullapool to Nantucket on the decks of the herring drifters – and that's when they were in harbour. Tomorrow there will be just one giant trawler purser seasooker that does for the lot of us. I heard of a crew that made a squillion each one night. They landed at a shady pier and quickly banked offshore. Real independence would include defence of biological resources held in common against our own and other pirates. Plus, to re-found our country properly, nationalisation of major minerals and bringing to book all tax-evaders.

A billionaire I schooled with wants to raze the ancient elms in a sunken classical garden to raise a shrubbish granitette hoohaa instead. The leader of a party not unadjacent to the ruling party in Scotland has been backing this aberration and Scottish Enterprise has largely paid for the relentless PR. The project to demolish Union Terrace Gardens is hailed by the exaggerators as *vital* and *transformational* when *fatal* and *deformational* would be nearer. A party that leads the call for independence would do well to wake up to its own whipped centralism.

Up the coast, a man with hair combed to the eyes, and shooting from the hip, rakes the marram out of the dunes to make a golf course. A party not unadjacent to the current ruling party in Scotland thinks this is grand and approvable and overrides the piffling independence of the local community to make it so. Billionaire then gives Combman an honorary degree and lauds him for *putting Scotland on the international golf map*. Fictionalists from St Andrews to Troon are made redundant because they could not make that up. Combman, imported patriot, then has a bad attack of wind. And a party that purports to trailblaze to independence should now dump a tendency to tatty diktats?

Trees for Life are engaged in restoring the Caledonian pine forest. Some of my best friends are Scots pines, so I go to help Trees for Life root out slump-shouldered sitka spruce and replant with bonny, red-barked, strong-limbed *Pinus sylvestris*. It is a slow process, as many good processes are. TfL are also campaigning to reintroduce the wolf to Scotland. The last one was killed in 1746 by a Highland hunter called McQueen. Imagine the ceremony, if youse will. *Scotland – I don't know if you still remember – this is Wolf. Wolf, meet Scotland.* What will the wolf think?

Meanwhile – another screengrab – as you stand in the centre of Inverness, an odd bus passes. Its destination board reads *Culloden via Tesco*. In the days before heritage got polish, if you went to Culloden, there was a wooden notice stuck in the heather which read: *Dangerous Battlefield – Wear Sensible Shoes*. After independence, but not before, that same bus will be re-routed past Braw Brogues, that we may suffer no such deficiency again. More pointedly, the TV documentary *Culloden* by Peter Watkins was made for buttons in 1964, with shivering, bloodied local folk, some of them battlefield descendants, recruited to do the dying. With a

Brechtian yet empathic authenticity both moving and thought-demanding, *Culloden* set a pellucid standard for antihype. But antihype is not really TV's country. And so after Watkins' *The War Game* the following year, a scorching exposé of how kitchen door shelters don't halt H-Bombs, TV dropped him.

Speaking of Armageddon, we are hanging on for the showdown...

As regards underworld, we once had three hundred years' worth of recoverable coal. I went down the Seafield Colliery for a visit, a mile down at the speed of darkness, three miles out under the Forth in the dripping tunnel on the man-riding train. Many of the folk in the Fife coalfield were practically communists. So that had to be closed down, the pits flooded, mainly by Thatcher. To recruit for independence, if it is to be more than *Uhuh* and a yawn, we might need to reinvigorate that deep sense of the commons?

Anent independence, most working people have none. The only power they have, if they are employed at all, is to withdraw their effort. This is not acknowledged by certain politicos, who can be spotted not on the picket line but hopping from studio to studio wringing their hands. Meanwhile capital can go on strike or abroad for as long as it likes whenever it pleases, and nobody holds it to account – there's independence for you. Indeed if capital catches cold from all its jaunting we purchase for it a medicine called *Independence Plus*. It is dispensed in a pail. As for one spoon of medicine for the rest of us, that would only encourage sloth and dependency. Before we write a prospectus for independence, I suggest we read and reread the recent works of David Harvey, Žižek and Badiou.

Because, with so-called *independence*, would the iron rule continue that capital needs its minimum 3% annual return, come what may? Even if it means laying tram tracks annually and tearing them up, scrapping human scale crew-owned fishing boats to build supercapitalistic ones, and rooting out beloved gardens to ram some architectural crassness over them? Or would we roll up our political sleeves in order to regain and develop our nationally-owned, locally-owned, and communally-owned sectors? Huge questions, perhaps only fully answerable in action, once the present interim independence-seeking party helps us get there and then splits. Rather grimly, in terms of portent, at the moment of writing the Scottish government has just awarded the Orkney and Shetland ferry contract away from the nationally owned NorthLink to those ubiquitous public contract snafflers Serco. So that by the time this is published, cuts in employment and employment standards will almost certainly have followed, to ratchet up Serco's margin.

Yet I applaud instances where this Scottish Government has been humane. The freeing of Abdelbaset al-Megrahi, tempering justice with mercy, and against the fierce denunciation emanating from the US State Department, was a noble moment in our history, nobler in the annals of virtue than even Bannockburn. Albeit his conviction in a Scottish court in the first place had hallmarks of superpower subornment. Just as, in our daily political life, a footloose international media mogul has been interfering too.

In a different sphere, I applaud the Scottish Government's removal of prescription charges, and hope it presages the maintenance of a full and proper National Health Service. But in March 2012 a die was cast on this matter in England. The UK coalition government, comprising two parties that, clapped-together, would barely form a rump in Scotland, forced through the Health and Social Care Bill against universal professional advice and a million petitioners, thus laying the whole health service in England open to usurpation. I travelled to Westminster to lobby against this, but the coalition had already sold its ears.

So up to 49% of beds in NHS Foundation hospitals in England are now legally available to be allocated to private patients. This will impact indirectly on Scotland as a Barnett consequential. The grant we receive for our hospitals from the annual Barnett formula pro rata block grant is calculated on what is received by English hospitals from government funding, but *not* from private insurance fees. Once the temporary arrangements made to cover this have faded, Scottish health services, unless we get a grip and do something, will haemorrhage grant and be driven in the same ghastly privatising direction.

Let me close with a confession. It is ever easy to be lulled by the spell of hype. In January 2009 I flew to Obama's inauguration, and hungrily allowed myself to come under the influence. At the start of the week I sang *We Shall Overcome* in Washington's National History Museum – linked in arms with African Americans who dared to hope that serious social change had come to pass. By the end of the week, back in New York, the neon high round News Corp's skyscraper was tickering: *President Orders Missile Attack on Afghan Village – 18 Dead.*

On the Amtrak train between these cities I talked with Americans. Was this a fresh chapter in their democracy? We talked of many things, principally *socialised medicine.* They wanted none of that nasty stuff. I said, *Forget the two-word dismissal: you need six words to understand the founding principle of the NHS. What are your six words?* rapped a sceptic. *Free at the point of need,* I said. I further claimed, indeed asserted, that the USA could never regard itself as a civilised country until it looked after the healthcare needs of all its citizens.

Dear reader, I got out alive. And that exemplifies the real basis on how I will vote – if spared – in the referendum in two years' time. I will vote to be in a better position afterwards to fight to keep the single greatest bedrock achievement of socialism and human decency we have: the National Health Service. And since I do not think the Electoral Commission will trouble to find peely-wally *Uhuh* in its vocabulary – and since the process of essay-making has cardioverted the caveats in my ageing heartbeat – I will make my vote count on the side of *our life,* and not for capitalism.

Yes, I will say, *Yes.*

ALLAN ARMSTRONG

The prospect of a referendum on Scottish independence has stimulated much discussion amongst Socialists. This essay sets the tactics and ideologies of the current campaign within long-standing debates on Scottish self-determination, going back to the end of the nineteenth century and the first national democratic challenges to the unionist state.

The 'Irish Revolution' which began in 1879 triggered a series of economic, social and political movements, which led to a questioning of the very existence of the UK. As a result, profound divisions emerged amongst the British ruling class over how best to maintain its rule over these islands and their wider empire. (See Allan Armstrong, *From Davitt to Connolly - 'Internationalism from Below' and the Challenge to the UK state and British Empire, 1879-95.*) Major economic and social struggles became linked to demands for national self-determination in Ireland, Scotland and Wales.

For most of the Scottish Left at the time, the best way of satisfying these demands was through Home Rule. This Home Rule policy had been devised by Liberal and Radical thinkers, but many other Liberals and Radicals joined with the Conservatives as Unionists to oppose constitutional reform. Yet, both Unionists and Home Rulers of the late-Victorian period supported the United Kingdom and British Empire. Together these were seen to be the very embodiment of the 'British road to progress' and an example to the whole world. Home Rule was, in effect, an alternative unionist version of this view.

However, in the course of the International Revolutionary Wave from 1916-21, the Glasgow revolutionary John Maclean addressed the issue of Scottish self-determination in a radically new way. From 1919, Maclean began to advocate political independence for Scotland. This was to take the form of a Scottish Workers' Republic, as part of the new World Communist order which seemed then to be advancing everywhere. Maclean's strategy involved the break-up of the UK and British Empire, which he saw as the major bulwark of the existing imperialist world order. However, the revolutionary wave ebbed, and the overwhelming majority of the Left, whether they were in the Labour, Independent Labour or Communist parties, settled for differing versions of a 'British road to socialism'.

This approach was but a contemporary projection of the nineteenth-century Liberal and Radical belief in 'the British road to progress'. Thus when it came to the issue of self-determination for the constituent nations of the UK, that old political divide amongst Liberals and Radicals – between the Unionists' constitutional status quo and the Home Rulers' constitutional reform – reared its head episodically on the Left also. As late as 1979, during the first Scottish devolution referendum campaign, this divide split and paralysed the Labour government of the day, ushering in a period of conservative unionist reaction under Thatcher.

Are we now seeing a demand for the type of Scottish independence that Maclean first raised, for independence against the British Union and Empire? The official debate on Scottish independence is certainly not being conducted in these terms. Instead, it represents an updated version of that older debate between Conservative Unionists and Liberal Home Rulers, but where these respective positions have been taken up by an alliance of Labour, Lib-Dems and Conservatives on one side, and the SNP on the other.

The SNP's 'Independence-Lite' proposals would leave any future Scotland still saddled with paying billions of pounds of debt (to which Scottish bankers massively contributed), a bloated military machine wasting billions on wars, and a top-heavy and very costly bureaucracy headed by a parasitical monarchy. The UK state would still be able to directly intervene in Scottish politics, since the Crown Powers would still be in place. These powers have even been used to topple elected governments [as Meaghan Delahunt's essay in this volume reminds us - *Ed.*].

'Independence-Lite' is but a modern continuation of that old Liberal Home Rule tradition. It could best be described as 'Independence within the Union' – a term originally coined by Scottish Labour's First Minister at Holyrood, the late Donald Dewar, and more recently repeated by the SNP's Education Minister, Michael Russell. This amounts to little more than draping all the key institutions of the UK state located in Scotland in tartan.

Furthermore, just as the old Home-Rulers accepted the wider British Empire, so the present SNP leaders are keen to uphold the current global imperial order. Salmond has been every bit as quick as Tony Blair to pander to the likes of Rupert Murdoch and Donald Trump. Indeed, Salmond believes that, given further powers, Scotland could be even more accommodating. It could become a low-tax haven for the global corporations. The SNP continues to loudly champion Scottish regiments' part in the wider British imperial and NATO war machine. Like those earlier Home Rulers, Salmond is desperate to reassure the current global masters that 'Independence-Lite' offers them no fundamental challenge. He represents a wannabe Scottish ruling class. Under no circumstances do the SNP's leaders want to mobilise any popular movement from below which could jeopardise their chances of future advance.

If Salmond was to be successful in getting a Yes vote on his terms, then possession, as they say, is nine parts of the law. The SNP government 'owns' the official Yes referendum campaign. Its political limits are firmly set by SNP support for big business, both Scottish and multi-national. This provides the SNP with a veto, as Labour had with the Scottish Constitutional Convention (SCC) that preceded its own 1997 Devolution Bill. And just as the SCC refused to have anything to do with the massive anti-poll tax revolt in Scotland, so the Yes campaign will take no part in the resistance to all cuts devised by Westminster, passed on by Holyrood, and implemented by both Labour and SNP controlled local councils.

Yet, 'Independence-Lite' is still unacceptable to most Unionists because it opens up some unpleasant prospects. Existing international treaties and alliances may need to be renegotiated. Scotland would have its own representation in the EU and the UN. Most disturbing of all, there could be a question mark over the status of a diminished or not-so-Great Britain, and hence the UK's seat on the UN's Security Council.

Because the issue of Scottish independence has international ramifications, Unionists (Labour, Lib-Dem, Conservative UKIP, BNP, SDL and EDL) are seeking backing throughout the UK for their anti-Scottish independence stance. Reactionary Unionists and Loyalists in Northern Ireland have indicated their strong support for the British Unionist campaign. Unionists will also seek official US support as a pay-off for the UK state's loyal commitment to all those imperialist wars.

This is why Salmond's political strategy for winning the Scottish independence referendum is to constantly dilute the meaning of self-determination to the point at which it becomes acceptable to the majority of the current Scottish establishment, and provides little threat to the British and US ruling classes. All the SNP government wants from the majority of Scottish voters is a suitably placed X in the Yes box on the referendum ballot paper in 2014. After that, things should just be left in their 'capable hands' to conduct the ensuing negotiations.

There are some on the Left who argue that Salmond should be given fulsome support in the Scottish independence refer-endum. By adopting 'Independence-Lite', they think that

Salmond is just 'boxing clever' to get a Yes vote, after which the gloves will come off. The same kind of thing was said when Tony Blair ditched Clause 4. Some claimed, at the time, that this was necessary to beat the Tories, but that after the 1997 election New Labour would have the large Westminster majority needed to implement fundamental changes. In the end, the victorious New Labour government did abolish a few of the most discredited Tory policies, but Blair (and Gordon Brown) actually intensified the neo-liberal onslaught.

Despite the illusions of some on the Left, there is little likelihood of any post-independence SNP dissolving itself to give way to new Right and Left parties. There is no historical precedent for this. Those nationalist parties that have led successful independence campaigns have had long life spans. Ireland, India and South Africa provide just some examples. Basking in the prestige of their independence victories, these parties are quickly 'colonised' by all those who want to join the aspiring ruling class. They use their wealth and influential outside backers to marginalise any perceived radical challenge within the party ranks. Looking once more to the New Labour precedent, the creation of Tony Blair's government did not lead to an organised Left challenge and split within the party. Ken Livingstone and George Galloway were expelled.

Others argue that after the independence vote, Scotland's 'natural' left-of-centre political culture can be relied on to make its influence felt. There are a number of problems with this. Scotland has not always been so left-of-centre. In the 1955 general election, Scotland gave the Tories an absolute majority of the vote. Radicalism is not some innate feature of the Scottish people. It took countless Socialist activists and many years of Socialist (or at least social-democratic) campaigning to move Scotland to a more left-of-centre position.

Amid such heady debates we can easily lose sight of the fact that social-democratic politics are currently in retreat throughout the UK, including Scotland. Whenever Labour or the SNP do make any social-democratic electoral promises, these are dependent first on capitalism's ability to maintain its profits. That has always been the nature of social democracy, and today we are living in times of mounting economic crisis. In such circumstances, for Labour and the SNP, bailing out the banksters is their first priority. The SNP may still be a little way behind Labour in its moves to the Right, but it is going down the same road.

If Socialists fail to develop an independent profile during the referendum campaign and link this with policies such as opposition to austerity, Trident, membership of NATO and participation in never-ending imperial wars, then Salmond will be free to decide who gains from any Yes vote. You can be sure the beneficiaries will be those to whom the SNP government feels really indebted – Sir Brian Souter, Sir George Mathewson, et al. After the 1922 Treaty with the UK government, the Irish Free State began to remove those welfare reforms inherited from the 1909 Liberal UK government and replace them with Catholic charity, once the Republican opposition had been defeated. The current SNP government certainly includes those who would see their future 'Scottish Free State' as an opportunity to privatise social services.

Failure to confront the SNP government will only ensure that, in the unlikely event of a referendum Yes vote being achieved by its chosen methods, power will be firmly entrenched with a new Scottish ruling class. Therefore, Socialists should use the referendum campaign not only to put forward a very different vision of an independent Scotland, but to link this up with all those resisting the current attacks on our class.

As a first step, there needs to be a campaign for a Scottish republic unconstrained by the UK's anti-democratic Crown Powers; independent of both the City of London and the European Central Bank (ECB); and removed from the British military machine. This means openly challenging those anti-working class forces, which the SNP government wants to keep on board.

A return to the idea and practice of Scottish self-determination first raised by John Maclean is required, but modified to address today's conditions. This means organising an Internationalism from Below challenge to the New World Order. To have some hope of achieving this, we need not 'Independence Lite' to benefit the SNP's business backers, but an 'Independence-Max' which can begin to empower us, provided we organise ourselves independently.

ALAN BISSETT

If there's a single image that describes the transformation Scotland went through during my childhood it is this: the fences all got bigger.

I grew up on a new-build housing scheme in Falkirk called Hallglen. In 1975, the year of my birth, my parents were among the first people to move there. It looked just like *Gregory's Girl*, the council homes gleaming an identical white. There were grass parks, ash parks, swing-parks, woodland, shops owned by local people, two bars, even a nightclub (which, I'm reliably told, attracted folk 'from as far away as Airdrie'). It was a great place to grow up, a testament to imaginative social housing. The fences were two feet high, which meant you could literally walk in and out of anyone's back garden. My memory of the early eighties was of parties: street parties, house parties, gala days, the adults rolling around singing the hits of the sixties and Corries songs, while their children were upstairs on the Atari.

Come the Nineties the fences were five, six, seven feet high. Nobody walked in and out of their neighbour's gardens. The street parties had stopped. Envy of neighbours became all-pervasive, and so the arms race: two cars per household, foreign holidays, TVs in every room, double-glazing, patios, garden extensions, conservatories, satellite dishes. It's not that there was no warmth or friendliness any more, but put it this way: people no longer come all the way from Airdrie to the pubs and clubs of Hallglen because nobody really bothers to leave the house anymore.

In 1975 the majority of people in Scotland were council house tenants. In 1992, after Right to Buy, my oldest group of friends defied their staunchly Labour parents and used their first votes to help return the Conservatives. Working-class boys, they believed the Tories were going to make them middle-class men, richer than their parents had been. They would've described themselves as proudly British, pro-Monarchy, anti-trade union. They believed that if you wanted it enough you got to the top, and if you didn't get there then it was probably your own fault. They became property owners as soon as the banks were willing to let them. A working class identity still meant something to them, but it wasn't an indication of where they wanted to *go*. They were, by any standard, Thatcher's Children.

It's funny, but a generation who were told that they were 'no longer working class' ended up doing an awful lot of work. My friends and family have toiled every day of their lives, whatever jobs they could find – night-shifts, back-shifts, split-shifts – kept their heads down and obeyed the system. If any of them found themselves on benefits they made every effort to get off again straight away. They are now saddled with enormous debt, just from wanting to live as everyone else did, and wracked by job insecurity. They are not comfortably middle-class. They are not even better off than their parents. Crippled by their mortgages they will be working for longer, and for a lower pension, than their parents did. Their own children face a highly uncertain future. Should they wish to complain about employment conditions they are told, 'Just be thankful you have a job.' They can't go on strike for longer than a day, because, well, *who's going to pay the mortgage?*

My friends' hatred of the rich is now palpable. It's not because they themselves didn't become rich, but because they've realised the system was rigged all along. Having rejected socialism for most of their adult lives, having rejected even the very *existence* of a working class, they now burn with fury at a system which purports to be meritocratic but which in reality works against them. Their arrival into the 'middle class' had been an illusion, sustained by easy credit and an economy which required conspicuous consumption to sustain itself. But where, in reality, are they now? They're still on square one, with the awareness that even square one may seem like a lovely mirage in a couple of years' time.

The scale of what is happening to people is enormous. We are only just beginning to catch up with the long-term effects of Thatcher's economic model, carried on grandly by New Labour and accelerated by the current Tory/Lib Dem coalition. After 1945 British people relished the future. Now they are scared of it. The disabled and the unemployed, despite the absence of work, are 'scroungers' again. Many who use this term fail to understand just how possible it is that they might be 'scrounging' in future. Meanwhile, a casual glance into restaurants in Central London on a Monday night will confirm that there are parts of the country which the recession has not touched.

Perhaps, then, we start to wonder why Scotland, an oil-producing nation, has some of the lowest life-expectancy in Europe. We might consider the McCrone Report of 1975, commissioned by the (Tory) Heath government, which showed that were an independent Scotland to nationalise its oil it would be one of the richest countries in the world. We might ask why Labour also buried the report. We are, after all, told to believe that Westminster acts in the best interests of the Scottish people.

In 2001 I was interviewed for a book called *Being Scottish*, edited by Tom Devine and Paddy Logue. I was 24 and so, in that irritating way young men often do, I made every attempt to be iconoclastic. 'Scotland barely exists any more,' I ventured, 'for people my age it's just the name we give to the place where we live.' Fast forward to May 2012, and there I am in Fountainpark Cinema, Edinburgh, part of the line-up for the launch of the *Yes Scotland* campaign, which hopes to persuade Scots to vote for independence in 2014. That's a strange about-turn, even allowing for the naivety of my youth. Most of my friends and family in Hallglen, the ones who were once 'proud to be British', intend to vote for an independent Scotland. Not everyone in Scotland is convinced yet, but I do think that most of them would like to be.

I can only speak for the people I know, but the seeds of our political awakening can be found in our refusal to consider 'Scotland', as it was, a polity in the first place. Unaware that we were being massaged by forces larger than ourselves, we believed Scotland to be a dustbin, self-destructive in its habits and negative in its outlook, unwilling to drop the infamous chip on its shoulder and get on with things. Scotland had a loser's mentality. Scotland was uncool. Scotland 'barely existed'. We were also the first generation utterly defined by what it consumed, fed from childhood a twenty-four hour barrage of advertising, brand names, screens. Think of popular culture between 1979 and 1990, Thatcher's reign: Star Wars merchandise, Hollywood action movies, glossy American soap-operas, video games, Sky television, Disneyland, MTV, McDonalds, Nike, Tesco, shopping malls. This was the dazzling face which replaced the brown, concrete late-seventies, the shower of sparkles that made Reaganomics and Thatcherism feel exciting. Commingling with this: English news, English sitcoms, English daytime shows, English football commentators, Royal weddings, Wimbledon, the Houses of Parliament and cricket. Even Rangers, the football team we supported, came draped in the Union Jack. Of course Scotland didn't exist! Where the hell *was* it? Scotland was 'just the name we gave to the place where we lived'.

I think back to times when a shot of what might be called Scottishness broke through and became something too real to be dismissed as 'uncool'. Fishing trips to the Highlands, surrounded by hills. Scotland defeating Sweden 2-1 in the 1990 World Cup. Ceilidh dancing and kilts at weddings. Hogmanays. *Braveheart*. Billy Connolly videos. *Trainspotting*. 'Flower of Scotland'. There we were, looking at ourselves, undeniable, a mirror in a world of windows. Scotland still existed.

These are supposed to be clichés, but the clichés are what nourished us in the absence of a full nation.

By the time I'd reached my thirties James Kelman, Alasdair Gray, Janice Galloway, Tom Leonard, Robert Burns, Peter Mullan, Lynne Ramsay, James Hogg, Liz Lochhead, Edwin Morgan, John McGrath, Iain Crichton Smith, Agnes Owens and Jimmy Reid had excavated through the surface of my Scottishness, hauling a class politics back up with them. But, if I'm being honest, most of these are still names largely unknown to the Scottish mainstream. If I'm being even more honest, I would have found very few them myself had it not been for the huge success of the film *Trainspotting*, abetted by a Britpop marketing campaign and the fact that heroin had become chic among the London glitterati. In short, the success of *Trainspotting* in London was the main reason why Scottish literature became visible to Scots. Do the French encounter their own culture so rarely? Do the Americans? Do the Chinese? Do the English? Scotland has existed, for most Scots, mainly in their subconscious.

And so when the SNP's colossal election victory of May 2011 was announced, as the scale of their achievement dawned, it was clear that something in Scotland was changing. We were *waking up*. Of all the 'most Scottish' things that I have ever felt this was by far the strongest. The lid had been lifted from the boiling saucepan. Suddenly my friends and family were all phoning each other. Are you seeing this? Are you seeing what's happening! Scotland is rebelling! *WE ARE SAYING NO!*

Trapped, trapped, and now freeing ourselves. A switch has been flicked. It's no doubt true that not everyone who voted SNP in the 2011 election wanted an independent Scotland. But they still voted for the Scottish Nationalist Party. At the very least, it was a rejection of Westminster and their choice of Coke, Pepsi and Diet Pepsi. At the very least, it was an awareness that Scottish Labour has effected no great change in the lives of people who've been voting for them, since they are being worked from behind by a party that still wants to appeal to Middle England.

It was still a rebellion. It was still a vote *for Scotland*. The potential in this country for real, peaceful, democratic change cannot be underestimated. Staunch unionists, of course, will exploit fear of economic collapse by imagining that an independent Scotland could not act to save itself. But to depend any further on the artificial construct of the United Kingdom is suicide, for all four countries within it. Britain is working this out. Scotland was the inception, but it's clear a realignment is taking place all over. Artists are often inclined to sense the nature of things coming over the hill, and it's significant that the National Theatre of Wales has commissioned a major play on 'independence' to coincide with Scotland's referendum in 2014. Wales is watching. They'll decide their own relationship with the rest of the 'United Kingdom' in due course, but they will be at least considering it. The English, who are largely convinced that Scotland could not possibly survive, will agitate against Westminster once they see an independent Scotland thriving. We could inspire the whole of the British Isles to become part of a larger European fightback. All of this is impossible to do within the Union. The best chance for British people is to dismantle the imperialist relic of the United Kingdom, created undemocratically by Scottish and English nobles in the first place, and reimagine the political landscape.

Already new shapes are emerging. We have the Occupy movement, increased industrial action, the election in Bradford of a party to the left of Labour, European voters beginning to reject austerity, Iceland protecting the Icelandic taxpayer by letting its private banks fail, even Barclays shareholders rebelling against obscene executive bonuses. These are diverse but linked phenomena. If the SNP fail to read this situation correctly they are doomed. An independent Scotland could become either part of this global justice movement or yet another means for multinationals to exploit local economies.

If the referendum is to succeed it will be because it has tapped into the thwarted hopes of that layer of people who'd supposedly entered the middle class in the last thirty years, but who've crashed back down again. They are the catalyst at this stage of Scottish history. The first thing we must do is re-admit the concept of a working class back into politics. This class not only never went away, given how many were left behind by both Thatcher and Blair, but is now expanding to include 'middle-class' people whose living standards have narrowed. The SNP vote has been a protest from these huge groups, which has brought us to the point of the referendum. But after being hammered by Thatcher and betrayed by Blair, Scottish people must be offered a powerful alternative vision, not a watered-down version of the same.

The received wisdom is that people will vote on the basis of economics, and that will no doubt be a large factor. But until 2014 this is what people will hear: the Unionists saying Scotland can't afford it, the Yes campaign saying we can. Most people are not economists and will be unsure who to believe. For the Yes campaign to be successful, Scots will need to recognise in it a sense of their own grievance. 'Anger,' as John Lydon once sang, 'is an energy'. We must talk the language of hurt as much as the language of hope. The so-called chip on the shoulder exists for a *reason*.

In a recent interview, Shirley Manson, the Scottish lead singer of the band Garbage, said she was 'vehemently against independence' because 'we should be tearing fences down, not building them'. Unconsciously, she's on the right lines. She's just misread the situation. The fences went up in the Eighties. Tearing them down is exactly what Scotland is trying to do.

JENNI CALDER

Sometimes, to amuse myself, I turn the map of Europe upside down. There is Cornwall in Britain's top right hand corner, and the Scilly Isles in a box, and in the bottom left Caithness, Orkney and Shetland (in a box). Britain no longer looks bottom heavy, no longer weighed down in the south by population and wealth. You can imagine people rattling downwards like balls on a bagatelle board, to be caught in little pens marked Manchester, Leeds, Newcastle, Glasgow, Edinburgh. A few will get to Aberdeen or Inverness, but the northern third of Britain will remain lean.

Scotland upside down shifts attention to her Scandinavian neighbours. Perth and Dundee seem to bulk larger, the North Sea more prominent, the English Channel diminished. North no longer seems the *ultima thule*, the terrain of rough and rugged people, historically hard to reach and resistant to control. It is an illusion, of course, but instructive nonetheless to reverse, from time to time, our perception of geography – which, in turn, reminds us that the governance of Scotland has always been problematic. It's part of what makes Scottish history so inter-esting and the Scottish nation hard to define (perhaps, though, no harder to define than other nations).

I was never taught Scottish history. I went to school and university in the United States and England. But then my chil-dren emerged from their Scottish high school with only patchy and nebulous notions of Scotland's past. Scotland has produced several generations who are largely ignorant of Scottish history beyond episodes that have emerged as signifiers, largely as a result of requiring the past to fit current perceptions of what we want it to be. In 2014 we will be 'celebrating' the 700th anniversary of victory at Bannockburn, having, I suspect, declined to mark the 500th anniversary in 2013 of a defeat that arguably had more significant consequences for Scotland. No doubt Barbour's 'freedome is a noble thing' will be much quoted, but with how much thought of whose 'freedom' and how it related to the nobility?

Democracy will always be a flawed system, but the first responsibility of a democratic government is to ensure that it functions as effectively as possible. Sometimes it seems that elections take place either in an historical wasteland or in an historical bubble. We are either disconnected from the past or eagerly embracing a manipulated version. We are asking people to make decisions about the future in the context of a vast historical and cultural deficit, for which we cannot blame Westminster – Scotland has proudly insisted on controlling her own education system. We are being encouraged to nourish ideas of self-determination at the same time as our expectations are severed from the ballast of the past and its cultural expression.

In Scott's *Guy Mannering*, Dandie Dinmont escorts young Bertram across the border from Cumberland into Liddesdale. They travel through a wild and desolate tract of land which, Scott says, appears designed by nature 'to be the barrier between two hostile nations', but it is not clear where the dividing line lies. Their route takes them along broken tracks through bandit country. They negotiate bogs, rivers and ravines, and fight off attack. Today's border wriggles its way diagonally across the stretch of hills that connects the Solway Firth with the mouth of the Tweed. It is the product of centuries of contention and not much logic. Most borders are like that: debateable, shifting, accidental, and imposing often artificial definitions of identity. When in the 1950s my family made our annual summer visit north, chugging along the A68 in our Standard 8, we always cheered when we crossed the border. Ah, Scotland! There was a sign to prove it. You need a sign. There is no change in terrain or language or the colour of the pillar boxes. The border we crossed was not territorial but emotional. It was to do with an idea of home learnt from parents, and a sense of attachment even though we children could scarcely understand the language spoken by our Aberdeenshire relatives. We had been taught to respond to difference – our shout of 'hurrah!' at Carter Bar signalled an embrace of identity in the face of much that was alien.

Alien. That's an experience that is useful for any country pondering independence. Considering the part played by Scotland in the British imperial enterprise, it is curious that there is so little evidence of payback. The legacy of Scotland's presence in the Indian sub-continent, in the Caribbean, in Africa is not conspicuous on our streets in the way that it is in London or Bristol or Bradford. It is odd that Glasgow, gateway to Scotland's imperial riches, is so different from Liverpool or Cardiff in this respect. And meanwhile we encourage our diaspora to return to the homeland and spend. The notion of homeland as a place, almost by definition, that forebears left reluctantly has become part of, almost at the heart of, our construct of the past.

Whichever way up you look at Scotland, it is full of borders and barriers determined by topography, the mountains and the water seen as vital ingredients of the national character (and the national drink). The Scottish mainland has nearly ten thousand kilometres of coastline. There are over 600 lochs and many hundreds of rivers and burns. Mountain passes define all Scottish journeys north of the Highland Line. A century after the Treaty of Union those mountains still signalled a wild place inhabited by a wild people, just as they had a century before the Union when James VI tried to tame both. And now two hundred years on we still live in an internally disconnected country, a fact that has been a preoccupation of Scottish writers from Scott to James Robertson. Scotland needs sustainable communication across its many borders, trains and buses, bridges and ferries certainly, but for a joined-up Scotland we equally need books and theatre, music and pictures. Creativity is the powerhouse of connection and identity.

So how creative is the Scottish nation and what's nationality got to do with creativity? How connected are we, with each other and with the rest of the world? How robust is the Scottish identity? The point about creativity is not to provide answers but to keep asking the questions, in new ways and in different contexts. Artists should not ever be satisfied, which is just as well as no system of supporting them is likely to be entirely adequate or appropriate. In spite of this lack of satisfaction, or perhaps because of it, the Scottish literary endeavour in the past couple of decades has been strikingly productive. Our living writers are sought after throughout the world, their work has challenged and entertained, and a few of them have proved extremely popular. Our dead writers are increasingly attracting the attention of overseas scholars and students. A conference on Sir Walter Scott held in Laramie, Wyoming in 2011, brought together a splendidly international array of academics, and even a few cowboys.

But writers, established and aspiring, still face many difficulties. Where are the sustainable magazines to give space to new writing? How can Scottish publishers retain their successful writers, inevitably lured by London money? What can dramatists do in the face of dwindling support for theatre companies? Why is it so hard to find Scottish books in Scottish libraries? How can writers find the space and time to do more than perfect their skills in drafting funding applications? But perhaps these are mere details in the broad and brilliant perspective of independence. Perhaps, released from Westminster, a Scottish government will turn a benevolent eye on its creative people, and on its children who do not yet know they can write and paint and sing, and on its teachers and librarians and academics, and say, right, folks, now you are free. And struggling writers will emerge blinking from their attics and cellars, their pockets stuffed with memory sticks, and all will be well. Ah, yes. Scotland is another country. They do things differently there (with due acknowledgment to an English author).

But... As it is currently formulated (and admittedly there is much that is misty or just missing) there is no hint or promise that independence will distance Scotland from the pressures and contingencies that affect the country's cultural life. And neither will it necessarily conserve and distribute more justly the nation's resources.

In Margaret Elphinstone's novel *Voyageurs*, an English Quaker crosses the Atlantic to search for his sister, who married a Scot working for the North West Company and then disappeared. She is doubly lost to the North American Quaker community she joined. Set in 1812, with the US and British North America on the brink of war, it has a great deal to tell us of borders and minorities, of language and identity, of exploitation and displacement, of endurance and dogged integrity. Scots are prominent in the tale, adventurous, ruthless, divided, comradely. The book is about dealing with threat and uncertainty, about risk and greed. It is by a Scottish woman, and published in Scotland. I would make it required reading in Scottish schools, and for all those intending to vote in 2014.

My grandchildren live in Penarth (look it up on the map). To visit them, I cross two borders. It's a journey I enjoy, taking me through the Southern Uplands and across the Solway, through Cumbria and Lancashire, and on to Shropshire and the Welsh Marches. You cross the Wye and as you descend to Newport you have the Welsh Valleys to the west. The valley coal made a Scottish fortune – you don't have to spend much time in Cardiff to spot the connection with Lord Bute. Scotland colonised? Ask the Welsh, or Canada's First Nations, or New Zealand's Maoris. My destination is the home of my son and his family who are a twenty-first century amalgam: Welsh, Irish, English, Scottish, Jewish and Iranian, with further connections to the United States, Lithuania, New Zealand and Kenya. What, I wonder, would an independent Scotland mean for my son, born in Nairobi, raised in Edinburgh and West Lothian, educated in Abercorn, South Queensferry, York and Cardiff, now working in Caerleon (you may want to look that up also)? How would it affect that journey I make several times a year, and the reverse journey he makes with his family?

In 1960 I was in Israel and ventured into the wasteland between East and West Jerusalem. Children played among the rubble and the remains of walls pock-marked with bullet holes. Israel and Palestine now live with the tragic legacy of that accidental border. In 1994 I made a journey by kombi (mini-bus) from Gabarone to Johannesburg. When we reached the South African border we had to get out of the vehicle and walk across a hundred yards of no man's land under the eye of armed guards. Borders, and indeed the very idea of nation, fill me with ambivalence, however interesting they are. I see little benefit in legislating for more permanent divisions. I'm a republican with a profound belief in the need to aspire towards social justice. So here's a thought. Britain has always marked itself as separate from the rest of Europe. As an island nation it has no external but many internal borders. Perhaps we are approaching Scottish independence from the wrong direction. Perhaps we are having the wrong debate. Perhaps the whole notion of independence, at least in the context of the UK, belongs to the previous century.

Scotland small? Hugh MacDiarmid convincingly said no, but nevertheless there is a bigger picture. That big picture could be a federalist Britain, acknowledging regional identities and ensuring functioning representation – bearing in mind that much of the north of England would be effectively disenfranchised by Scottish independence. This, I believe, could create something positive out of Britain's fragmented and discordant past, and might even offer new possibilities for our social and cultural future.

BOB CANT

The Scotland of my childhood can best be seen in the photographs of Oscar Mazaroli. He never visited the Angus farm where I grew up but the local community shared many of the characteristics of the places he did visit. The central unifying feature was hard work; both men and women worked, separately and usually on different tasks. They had a tempestuous relationship with the land that they worked; sometimes the land had the upper hand and sometimes the humans did. Education was valued and pleasure was disavowed, except for two or three ritual days of the year. The values that people lived by were determined by an authoritarian church. These communities were self-contained and people from five miles away were perceived as foreign. Anyone who wanted to explore homosexual desire honestly was treated as a misfit and ostracised or expelled.

People did want to explore homosexual desire and for that they had to make a journey. In the post-war years, many followed the example of the artists Robert Colquhoun and Robert MacBryde in making the journey to London, where homosexual people could find some space for themselves in the anonymity of the metropolis. Those who did not have the wherewithal to leave the country made their way to the nearest city on a Saturday night. In all Scotland's major cities, there was a bar within easy reach of the bus station or the rail station where homosexual men could drink discreetly with one another. The Glass Bucket, only a few hundred yards from the Dundee bus station, had such a reputation but I was always too scared to cross its threshold.

It's a different world now. All the old certainties have gone and a culture that values individual human rights has emerged in the changing social landscape. Since the Scottish Minority Group was first set up in 1969, various campaigns have made the case for the removal of the legal barriers that inhibited the lives of homosexual people – or, to use today's unpoetic parlance, lesbian, gay, bisexual and transgender (LGBT) people. The age of consent has been equalised; discrimination at work has been outlawed; service providers cannot refuse services to people because of their sexuality; same sex couples can enter civil partnerships and adopt children. These are achievements that the early gay rights activists could only have dreamed of. The legal pre-conditions for equal citizenship have been established but while there is now something approaching a level playing field it's not entirely clear that all the players accept the change of rules.

At this point in the article, I am going to start using the term *queer folk*. It is, like LGBT, a shorthand term for groups of people who do not, for one reason or another, conform with the hetero-sexual norms of society. I understand why it is important to have an accountable and inclusive shorthand term like LGBT that can be used in relations with public bodies but that is the limit of its usefulness. It is certainly not a term that evokes the very intimate parts of our personal lives. There are, of course, difficulties about the term queer because it has a history of notifying bigotry, but terms can be reclaimed and re-shaped. Queer, for me, is fluid and imaginative; it suggests a willingness to accept differences and cross boundaries; that lack of tidiness goes some way to reflecting the way that people actually live their lives.

Not everyone is happy about the ways in which queer folk are re-shaping their lives. Once people decide to come out as queer (or whatever term they use to describe themselves), there are those who respond in anger or resentment about what should be a fairly straightforward act of self-determination. When queers were hidden away in pubs like the Glass Bucket, they could safely be ignored. But all this coming out – now consolidated by legal backing – really is something else.

The most notorious expressions of anger and resentment against queer folk came at the turn of the century when Wendy Alexander (then Communities Minister) sought to repeal Clause 28 of the Local Government Act (1988), which prohibited the promotion of homosexuality in schools. All hell broke loose at this attempt to ensure that schoolchildren were able to access information about the sexuality of a considerable minority of the population. Adverts on billboards and buses urged people who wanted to protect children to 'keep the clause'. The country endured months of publicity that appeared designed to promote hatred of homosexuality; women in Glasgow reported incidents where people, quoting these adverts, verbally and physically harassed them because they believed they were lesbians. The campaign culminated in an unofficial referendum and those of us who used public transport found that we were paying for it through our bus fares. But while the campaign to Keep the Clause was unsuccessful in a legal sense, one of its successes was that it made it very difficult for politicians to talk openly about further reforms for a number of years. The hateful law had gone but the Scottish tradition of silence about homosexuality was confirmed in the public domain and most of the subsequent legal reforms emerged from Westminster.

Despite the fact that homosexuality is older than Christianity, some religious leaders have been outspoken in their denunciations of everything queer. The Roman Catholic Church has, particularly since Pope John Paul II equated approval of same-sex marriage with the toleration of evil, been relentlessly hostile to legislation removing barriers for queer folk. But while the Roman Catholic Church in England made some nuanced noises in 2011 indicating some acceptance of civil partnerships, the Scottish branch has remained positively Knoxian in its authoritarian resistance to change.

A decade after the bus-fare referendum, the level of debate

on queer issues seems more relaxed. Polls show that over 70% of Scots have positive attitudes towards queers and believe that prejudice against them should be tackled. An effective campaign in favour of marriage equality is currently underway and is notable for the high profile of youth organisations such as the Scottish Youth Parliament, LGBT Youth Scotland and the National Union of Students. Old-style gay liberationists such as myself have difficulties with the enthusiasm for what we used to call a bourgeois patriarchal institution but we also have difficulties with legalised inequalities and so we tend to support a demand that seems to have struck a chord across the world.

Research by Stonewall Scotland shows that abuse and violence is still a common occurrence for queer folk. 61% of those surveyed for their Community Safety Study in 2010 said that they felt unsafe on the streets and 16% felt unsafe at work; 68% of young queer people had been homophobically bullied at school; only 37% of the victims of homophobic crime in Edinburgh had reported it to the police. There is a considerable mis-match between legislative advances, expressed views of the general public and the recorded experiences of the queer population. The discovery of sexuality and the exploration of its meaning are challenging for all young people. All that much harder for young people seeking to reach an understanding of whether or not they are queer, particularly if they are growing up in a small town with no queer meeting places or attending one of the 79% of schools which have no policy on homophobic bullying. What will such young people make of remarks by Cardinal Keith O'Brien when he compares same-sex marriage with the legalisation of slavery? There is still some way to go before queer people can fully trust the rest of society to respect the equality of their citizenship.

There are all kinds of theories about prejudiced and violent behaviour against queers. It must surely relate to the crisis of masculinity in a society where men's identities, which were largely determined both at home and in the community by their experience of work, have been cut adrift. Now that the old industries have gone, the banks have been shamed and the model of the fighting Big Man has been diminished since the defeat of the miners' strike, there continues to be a vacuum in relation to socially acceptable expressions of masculinity. Recent legislation about sectarian behaviour at football matches seeks to challenge one particular manifestation of troubled masculinity. Suicide figures from the General Register Office of Scotland show that the suicide rate among young men stands at 31 per 100,000, as opposed to 17 per 100,000 in England and Wales. All this suggests a lack of hope and purpose, a lack of dialogue, a lack of narrative that they can call their own. In this context, it is not absurd to see homophobic violence as being motivated by envy against queer people for having a narrative of hope.

In the short to medium term, broad-based initiatives, similar to the Ben Cohen Stand Up Foundation in England, will emerge to challenge the bullying culture in schools, in workplaces and on the streets. The early days of the HIV epidemic revealed that when homophobic prejudice emerges, Scottish people have the capacity to express solidarity with the victims of such abuse. Once the rather more straightforward issue of marriage equality has been settled, it is to be hoped that the young queer activists will begin campaigns to root out expressions of homophobia in schools and in popular culture. In the 1970s, Rock Against Racism may not have eradicated expressions of racism from mainstream youth culture but it helped to make anti-racism first of all cool and then normal. It provides a valuable model for grassroots campaigns that seek to effect cultural change.

In the longer term, any initiative to generate hope has to engage with the whole population of Scotland. There can be no return to the workplace patterns portrayed by Mazaroli back in the 1950s and 60s but the benefits of full employment must be recognised and acted upon. Employment in the modern world need not determine personal identities, as once it did, but it should provide space for people to develop their own identities and their own values. A programme of investment in a sustainable infrastructure, in energy provision, in schools, in health services and in affordable childcare would help to generate the demand that would make the economy grow. It would bring back hope into the lives of the citizenry. It would, in short, be a New Deal for Scotland. If there were a nationalist government in power, it would probably be described as a nation-building programme; if there were a Labour government in power, it would probably be described as a society-building programme. Whatever constitutional settlement is agreed, the New Deal would be the element that would generate a narrative of hope in the everyday lives of all Scots.

The world economy is currently dominated by austerity fundamentalists. Some of these buffoons even favour changing national constitutions to outlaw the possibility of governments adopting demand-enhancing Keynesian policies. This will not work and within a few years there will be a realisation, probably following violent unrest, that growth with social justice is the only way out of economic chaos. Today, Scots politicians have the option of supporting austerity or supporting New Deal measures. They have a responsibility to argue the case for solutions that will re-energise the Scots economy and Scots society.

If a New Deal is introduced in Scotland, it will represent an opportunity rather than an entitlement. It will be an opportunity for Scots to work together to bring hope back into the everyday lives of the citizenry. For queer people, it represents an opportunity to participate openly in their own society; it also represents an opportunity for them to generate a profound cultural shift that does not tolerate prejudice. They can help to make anti-homophobic behaviour first of all cool and then normal.

Meanwhile, we should be searching for a latter day Mazaroli to record the everyday lives of Scots building a world where queer folk are part of the picture.

Marks and Spencer are trying to persuade me to buy a Madeira cake.

Madeira cake with union-jack icing. And shortbread in a tin shaped like a London double-decker bus. And a biscuit tin with the Queen's head on it. They seem to assume there's something I want to celebrate. Something to do with being British. Something to do with the Queen. Well thank you Mr. Marks. And thank you Ms. Spencer. And how wonderful this dear old lady has been doing her job so well for so many years. (Do you know if she's thinking of retiring?)

Please understand: this is not a criticism. I know you have your shareholders to consider. And that they demand your sales grow year by year by year and that you therefore keep needing to produce more and more merchandise to try to satisfy the insatiable black hole of the world financial system. In that way you're just like the rest of us: helpless slaves of the market. Of economic forces none of us are able to control or understand or bring to a halt. You remind me a bit of my mother-in-law. She's an admirable woman who's worked hard all her life and tried to do her best by the world. Her heart's been wearing out, as machines always do, and economic systems as well, and has been functioning less and less efficiently.

Those of us who loved her could see what was coming: we knew she had to change her ways and prepare for a day when her heart would simply no longer function. But she refused to listen. And now she's in a geriatric ward. She doesn't understand how she got there and none of us can see any way out. One neighbour weeps all the time and never says a word. The other is forever calling out for long dead relatives to come and help her. But they can't, of course. Being dead.

They remind me of the European Central Banks and the IMF: lamenting the loss of old prosperities and forever trying to apply remedies that may have worked in the past. But not now. But they hold onto them, because they seem to represent old certainties. In desperate times, even hard words like 'austerity' and 'balancing the books' seem to have a comforting ring, somehow.

It's not just the economy lying in the geriatric ward. Most of our ideas about the world and most of the ways we try to live in it are in the same condition. Old, worn out, tired: no longer fit for a changing world. We are utterly bound to an oil-based economy even though we know reserves are running out and even though we know using them increases the level of carbon dioxide in the atmosphere to a dangerous and deadly degree. We know there is a connection between this and climate change. For a while this seemed to affect only a few islanders in the midst of the Pacific ocean, or a few hundred million people in distant and low-lying countries like Bangladesh.

But we could cope with that. Buying a new car or installing a new central heating system seemed more of a priority. As did the new flat-screen TV. But now we know our own climate is changing in wildly unpredictable ways.

But we cannot change the way we live.

We are tempted to turn to atomic power to sustain our lifestyles: but we know this, too, is vulnerable to natural forces far stronger than ourselves. We saw the tsunami destroy the power station in Fukushima. Even the few consequences we know about are enough to terrify us: never mind those that are kept hidden from us. I keep thinking of words I wrote way back in 1985, in *Losing Venice*:

You remember the story our teacher told.
Of the wise man who built his house upon
the rock and the foolish one who built
his on the sand? We built ours on the mud.
We compromised.
And now we are sinking.
Year by year the tide water rises.
Already it has flooded our cellars;
Soon it will beat against our doors.
Then the waves will come and wash us
from the face of the earth.
The clouds gather. The storm is rising.
And it will come. Nothing can stop it.
We know. We laugh when we can;
We live, as we must.
Fear eats away our hearts. Will it spare us,
We wonder, will it spare our children?
Yet what can we do? Tear down our city?
Label the stones and move them, stone by stone,
Rebuild them on the higher ground?
All our energy is taken up with living.
Besides, is there any mountain high enough
to hide us,
Is there depth enough in any cave?
I doubt it. Crying is easy.
Laughter requires a little more strength.

What I meant by those last words, I think, is that we should try the best we can to avoid giving way to despair and keep hope alive in our hearts. And that art has a role to play in that.

I know from experience that my capacity to create art has saved me from self-hatred and despair. My work with other transsexual people in helping them find their creative voice has also demonstrated, time and time again, that creativity is a powerful force for the oppressed.

In my own work I consistently try to be unfashionably hopeful; I see each play as a little act of resistance against the despair industry of the media that so endlessly tries to disempower us.

Even though it is hard to keep hope alive when the levers of power are often so rusted, so corroded and corrupt; and when every politician knows that it would be political suicide to carry out the changes required.

What's more, we are part of a country that apparently regards it as fundamental to its safety and identity to possess weapons of mass destruction however grotesquely expensive they may be. And however absurdly inept. Whether they are nuclear submarines that run aground on sandbanks or aircraft carriers that have no aircraft, no-one in the political establishment seems able to see them as anything but crucial to 'Great Britain' or the 'United Kingdom'.

The truth is obvious: we are part of a disunited kingdom whose other title really should be Insignificant Britain. Mediocre Britain. Living delusionally in the past Britain. Suffering false memory syndrome Britain. Britain stranded in the geriatric ward of history. A terminal case.

So what do we do? How do we resist as we struggle at the same time to get to grips with the massive unavoidable changes that need to take place within ourselves and the way we perceive the world?

To realise that genetics turns our common understanding of medicine into something completely outdated. To begin to grasp that our understanding of the universe as a piece of Newtonian clockwork no longer fits the facts. To try to encourage our imagination and intellect to understand what relativity means. Try to get to grips with the fact that our traditional views of what makes a man a man and a woman a woman are of very little use at all. In other words we have to try to stop being flat-earthers.

But then so many people still are. It's all too easy for the need to change to fill us with fear; and for the fear to make us cling on to old certainties. Whether they're the Bank of England, the Mother of Parliaments, the literal truth of the Holy Bible or the Treaty of Union.

You could argue that in the context of everything else this is pretty trivial stuff. And how dismaying the fright of many people scared to move on from it. How contemptible that no-one seems to be capable of coming up with a single positive reason to remain in the Union. The only arguments its supporters seem able to muster are fear. Fear of losing our credit rating. Fear of border controls. Fear of losing the monarchy. Fear of losing defence contracts. Fear of change.

Can we really not find just a tiny bit of courage? Does it really make sense to stay attached to England? To a failing state governed in the interest of the City of London with its tiny coterie of obscenely wealthy bullies, thieves and robbers? A state hopelessly stuck in dreams of past glory, forever trying to 'punch above its weight', humiliatingly stuck in a self deluding 'special relationship' with its colonial master, incapable of creating any positive vision of its future?

My dear mother-in-law used every ounce of imagination and strength to deny the changes old age was forcing upon her. It did her no good at all. Change is coming, whether we like it or not.

Let's try, even if in our own small and insignificant way, to do our best to embrace it.

MEAGHAN DELAHUNT

When I first moved to Scotland twenty years ago, I was struck by the beauty of the place and the starkness of life here. I worked long, low-paid hours as a shop assistant. The summer months bore no resemblance to any summer I had ever experienced. Scots would shake their heads at me in disbelief: how could anyone in their right mind choose to leave Australia? *What are ye doing here? Don't ye miss it?* They meant the sunshine and the material comfort of *Neighbours* or *Home and Away*. This was a Scotland still smarting from the poll tax and Thatcherism, the destruction of heavy industry, mining villages and unions and I understood what they meant. Sometimes, on a dreich day, I shared their sentiments. But I also understood them as a form of 'cultural cringe', something oddly familiar from the Australia of my childhood.

How could a person migrate to such an outpost? A place so far away from the Centre? Generations of artists and writers before me had grown up with a sense of Australia not being important. They'd imbibed a colonial inferiority complex. They'd been flattened by the long white shadow of Australian history, the First Fleet notion that it was *terra nullius* – an empty land. There was a sense that anything worth happening was happening elsewhere, usually in the Queen's name, most often in London. Australia was *a godforsaken place, a cultural desert*: whether they saw it this way or not, many felt no option but to leave. The 'cultural cringe' of a nation always stems from a sense of powerlessness, a lack of self-determination, a lack of true freedom. I see this in Scotland, but I also see that it is changing. The 'cultural cringe' lost its power in my lifetime because we had political and cultural upheaval in Australia – a progressive government in the 1970s which forever altered our world-view and artists and writers prepared to stick their necks out. The same is now on the cards for Scotland.

Australia is still not fully independent, however, and 'the cultural cringe' seems to have morphed into its opposite, re-emerging as jingoism draped in a dodgy flag. This hit me with force on Australia Day this year, January 26. My sister had sent through a video link. *It's a shocker*, she assured me. In Scotland, it was still Burns Night. These two dates, coming so close together, always give me pause. January 26 is contentious in Australia. For many it is blighted, marking the 'discovery' of Australia for the British Empire, the genocide of Aboriginal people and a vision of the first white settlers being marched ashore in chains. For Indigenous Australians it is seen as 'Invasion Day'. I prize the fact that Burns Night celebrates a writer, not an act of war. Of course, Burns Night is not an official holiday and Scotland is not independent and who knows what we'll officially celebrate when we become so. I say 'we' because after 20 years here, despite being Irish-Australian, I definitely feel 'Scottish by formation', to paraphrase Muriel Spark.

But I digress. I click on the link. The video is called *'Straya Day* and it is, as my sister promised, *a shocker*. So bad it's good and I have to watch it twice. It depicts Australia Day as an overwhelmingly white, beer-fuelled blokefest. Flags adorn cars, bodies, faces, front lawns. The voiceover is racist, sexist, homophobic and takes the piss, big time. It was made by a disgruntled New Zealander and I salute the effort. We could dismiss this depiction of a few drunk, uneducated 'bogans' mouthing off about migrants, refugees, gays and Blacks as not representative. But even the current Labor Prime Minister, the daughter of Welsh immigrants, has a poor record of defending asylum seekers, migrants and the rights of Aboriginals. Sadly, I concede that the *'Straya Day* satire, both funny and disturbing, reveals the deeper truths of Australia's origins, wrapped up in a flag that is not wholly our own. This is 'cultural cringe' turned into its seeming opposite – a belligerent, hollow, national boast.

It's not inconceivable that this could emerge in Scotland. Indeed, we see it in embryo form already – in the kilts and shortbread and Scotty-dog versions hawked by the tourist board, in the 'Best Small Nation in the World' posters at Edinburgh airport. In the absence of real Independence all we have to fall back on are the white, male stereotypes of before. Where are the women, the immigrants, the writers, the artists? In short, where is the place for the 'other' when the 'cringe' manifests as jingoism?

The video gets me thinking about what Independence means and what a nation's flag represents. As a kid, Australia Day meant the last long weekend of the summer holidays. It meant jumping the sprinkler in the backyard, waiting for the barbie to heat and calamine lotion on the sunburn. There was little soul-searching but no flag-waving in the suburbs either. It was merely another glorious long weekend in the land of the long weekend. These jingoistic displays are relatively new. And whose flag are my compadres flying, I wonder, in a country which still has the Queen – an unelected, absentee Englishwoman – as Head of State? It is, undeniably, a *colonial* flag: a Union Jack with a scrappy Southern Cross in one corner. From there my outraged thoughts run to the Queen and her representative, the Governor General, and why Australia after all this time still isn't yet a republic, then to Scotland and the monarchy and what kind of independence we would want here. What flag would be flying? A Union Jack with a thistle underneath? 2012 is, of course, the year of flag-waving in the UK. The trifecta of the Jubilee, Olympics and arch Tories should mean that the SNP can kick back, enjoy, and watch the case for independence grow ever stronger. But in hard times bread and circuses have a diabolical allure, and this year might not be any exception. Where is the republican voice, I ask myself? More specifically, where is the Scottish republican voice?

In Australia, after a decade in the wilderness, the republican movement plans to act on Jubilee fatigue with events and education campaigns around the country. The 1999 republic referendum faltered over whether the Head of State should be elected by politicians or the people. This divided the republican vote, but they are making a comeback. In Scotland there is no comparable movement and Alex Salmond's 'personal affection' for the Queen does not encourage debate. (The SNP-led Scottish Government has even created a free 'Queen of Scots' iPhone app commemorating the Diamond Jubilee.) We are looking at a post-independence Scotland which retains the Queen as Head of State and ties us to the dubious colonial past. In this regard, the events of recent Australian history have something to tell us.

In 1972, Australians finally voted Prime Minister Robert Menzies and his Liberal Party (Tories) out of office. Imagine Thatcher in power for 23 years and you get the gist. Even as a kid I felt the excitement when the new, radical, Labor government came into power. Their campaign slogan was 'It's Time!' They were young, they were smart, and they spoke in our tongue, not in the strangled locutions of the Queen's English. Under Prime Minister Gough Whitlam a new era opened up of equal pay for women, Aboriginal rights, gay rights, free education, Medicare and support for the Arts. There was talk of closing American nuclear bases and the prospect of truly becoming an independent nation. Of course, none of this pleased Westminster or Washington and by 1975 powerful interests were working to destabilise the Labor Government. This led to what was known as 'The Dismissal', a constitutional coup in which the Governor General used his reserve powers on the Queen's behalf to dissolve Parliament and 'sack' Whitlam. Hundreds of thousands of people protested in city streets; the Army and the Navy were put on high alert and Australian democracy was fatally undermined. There was an unfortunate precedent for this. The Governor General had used reserve powers before – to dismiss State Premiers in 1916 and 1932. But to dismiss a *federally elected Australian Government*? My parents, indeed a whole generation, never fully recovered from the sense of betrayal in 1975, the sense of not being in charge of their own destiny. *May God Save the Queen*, intoned Whitlam, *for nothing will save the Governor General*. Children were sent home from school early as revolt was in the air. Whitlam told us to *maintain our rage* but most politicians, union leaders and above all, the press told us to calm down, keep order and vote for stability. A few years earlier, Murdoch had supported Labor. After the coup and the media hate campaign, my father burnt every Murdoch 'rag' he could find in the backyard incinerator and cancelled all subscriptions. People in Australia were left confused and uncertain by the speed and brutality of events, and, shortly after, an election returned the Conservatives to power.

What are the lessons here for Scotland? It's clear that we will pay a heavy price for reliance on Queens and media barons. The SNP policies on Trident call to mind Whitlam's challenge to American bases. The distribution of oil reserves, moves to shore up the welfare state, free education and health care for Scots – already these policies are so far to the left of what is happening in England as to seem a threat to the established order. Democracy and Constitutional Monarchy are fundamentally incompatible. The monarchy ties us to a class-riven, sectarian past and ensures that our relations with other countries (including Australia) are mired in that past. We need to keep hammering these points, even if it is a Jubilee Year, even if the SNP is intent on the long, canny game. We have to keep asking questions, for our official National Day will soon be upon us. We must be ready. Whose flag will we be flying? How will our 'cultural cringe' manifest? What kind of Scotland will we celebrate?

DOUGLAS DUNN

English. A Scottish Essay

I didn't choose you, nor did you choose me.
I was born into a version called Accent.
I haven't lost it, nor could it lose me –
I own it; it owns me, with my consent.
Some of my words were Playground. Others, though,
Came straight from an indigenous long ago
Out of old mouths in sculleries, or learned
Hanging around byres. Spoken, unwritten nouns,
Strong verbs, swept out of classrooms, overturned
Their fingerwagging mockery and frowns –
'*Speak properly*!' A 'Scottish education' –
Groomed to profess complexities of nation
In an amended tongue, while writing verse
In ancient cadences and noise, my voice
A site of rebel mimicry, its burrs,
Slurs, Rs, its sly, involuntary 'choice'.
    The wireless gave me safety, bield and space
To fill my room with music's commonplace
Sound for itself, not meaning. Moving dials
Across jazz and concertos, I cleared off
From the parish across a neutral aerial's
Invisible bridge. I couldn't get enough
Meaningless babble's radio-polyglot
Valve-busting links to Rome and Camelot.

Arthurian radio! Imagination!
Through knob-turned atlases of noise I found
Another and unfathomable nation
So overheard that it was underground.
Radio Inchinnan! Radio Renfrew!
Can you still hear me? Am I getting through?
That nation's called Poetry. It's policed
By Muses, not by critics, theorists, nor
Chief Constables hyping a long-deceased
National Bard as the forevermore
'Authentic' measure of the way to write
Poetry grounded in archaic hindsight
And retrospective fame, the Robert Burns
Syndrome. – 'Just write like him, and you'll be true
To Scotland when its good old self returns.
Then you'll be true to us, and true to you.'
Why do I disbelieve it? Why do I feel
It harms both mine and Burns's commonweal?
Because I do? Is it instinctive only
To think and feel the language I write in
Selects me to be snapped at, and feel lonely
When it's the tongue I know, that I delight in?
English I'm not. As language, though, you're mine,
Disinterested, Scots, also benign,
Or so I try to make you, keeping time
On beats of Burns and Shakespeare, Pope and Frost,
Plundered affinities, rhythm and rhyme
From any place or time and intercrossed,
MacCaig with Milton, Stevenson with Keats,
Byron, Browning, scanning the nationless beats.
    Not nationality but language. So,
What's odd or treacherous other than the name?
Not that I *like* the name – all my *bon mots*
In somewhere else's tongue! Why scourge and blame
History for what had to happen in it

When you can't cancel it, not by a minute,
Not by a year, never mind an epoch?
Go back, reclaim the past, to when we spoke
Each one of us as quintessential Jock?
Where, when, was that? Who were these purer folk
Whose tongues absolved them from an 'English' stain
And wrote their poetry in a native grain
So aboriginal its recited truth
Sang nation and confirmed a State from one
Infatuated lyrical in-love mouth,
A great God-help-us not-to-be-outdone
Embrace of who the Scots are, or might be,
Massive mouthpiece of *national* poetry?
No one – thank God! For we've got three sound tongues
In which to utter poetry, and three
Good reasons, therefore, for our native songs
To triplicate our nationality.
My Muse is mine alone; but still, she's free
To join her sisters in their choir of three,
If she should want to, and, if she should not,
She'll get her dander up if you accuse
My Lady she's an insufficient Scot –
She's not a politician, she's a Muse!
That sacred girl insists work be exact,
True to the spirit, measure, and the fact.
    What happened happened, though – 1707,
To go no farther back than that loud date.
Half understood, denied, or unforgiven,
It's not my number and it's not my fate.
The past's an interesting cadaver;
But let it rot. Don't let it stink for ever
Somewhere at the foot of the garden, or,
Worse, in your head. *Get that skull out of here!*
Rip all old pages off the calendar!
Try cranium-scrape, but get your head in gear!

– A memo to myself, to fight the ghost
Who steps from disappointment and distrust.
I've seen him sleeping on the 95,
Tricorned, peruked, an eighteenth-century gent,
Grave-robbed but looking very much alive,
A fierce old cove of the Enlightenment.
Damn *Braveheart*. It's the mind, not pikes and swords
Or martyred schiltrons but well-chosen words
Turn time around, direct it on ahead
Instead of back to where the clocks are stopped,
Stopwatches held in the hands of the dead.
When backs were stabbed and the secrets shopped,
Whisperers served the cause of trade. – A spit,
A wink, a shake of hands, and that was it.
Signed, sealed, delivered, to themselves, to them,
To us – Great Britain, that convenient phrase,
A rhotic, tri-syllabic nasty poem
Invented by a Treaty, tuned to praise
Union, aggrandizement, possession, money,
An archipelago of gluttony.
      Lists of neurotic Scotticisms; earnest
Desires to write and speak like Englishmen;
A wilful limpness in the national wrist –
Heyday of Edinburgh elocution!
But on the streets and closes Scotticisms
Meant nothing to apprentices and besoms.
Law Lords and luminaries spoke Braid Scots
Although when such as Kames sat down to write
Memorials or aesthetics, subtle thoughts
Found their expression in an erudite
Capital-city eighteenth-century prose
As natural to him as his daily brose.
Braid Scots was prose-less in Lord Kames's time.
Abundant prose there was, but not in Scots –
Although not pre-prose, Scots prefers to rhyme,

Foxed by the plots and counterplots
Of history – 1603, 1707,
Those dates by which our languages are driven.
Ramsay, Ross, Fergusson, and balladeers
Wrote their full-throated oppositional poems
For native minds and aboriginal ears
To reassert the sound of vocal home's
Domestic noise, the tongue of a *patrie*
Wagging and singing, almost a refugee
In the mouths of its speakers, and pathos
Beginning, the sorrow of movement, shifts
In time as change became perceived as loss
And what came in instead felt less than gifts
Between tongue and teeth, but as something fake.
A foreign language for men on the make
In London or Calcutta, Hudson's Bay,
British regiments, enslaved plantations,
Or on the London stage in 'the Scottish play',
Banks and Westminster, the British nation's
Class-lingo infiltrated 'social stations' –
Legged up by legover. Intimate unions
Ran parallel before the paper Act
In Anglo-Scottish sexual communions
Where love and love of property, the fact
Embedded snugly in commercial chance,
Led straight to land, preferment, and finance.
    Historical amusement, not treachery
In that careerist scramble, changing tongues
With the polished skills of sonic forgery
And climbing up the social ladder's rungs
By each perfected step of mouth – 'station'
Determined by 'correct' pronunciation!
As well forget or turn a blind eye on
Ancestral roguery, so far back it's
A shoulder diehard dreaming Tories cry on.

Best, though, to know your past, then call it quits,
For if you don't you'll Balkanise your brain
Or Irish it with history's inhumane
Serbianisms, ethnic cleansing's dire
Epic revenges for events before –
Hundreds of years before – present desire
And possible fulfilment. MacMinotaur
Lurks in this labyrinth, sectarian,
Preening his tammy, polishing his grin.
    Haar settles on the mist-dimmed coast of Fife.
St Andrews Castle's introverted stone
Withdraws into its tended afterlife.
July's inertia's a Scotophone
Sensation as I wander round the walls
All ears for ghost-words, listening to my pulse
Tapping to blood's stone history as speech,
Knox and Fife's local lairds, in English pay,
Defending this, Knox taking time to preach
Despite the shot of French artillery.
An archaeologist of wrathful breath,
I recreate his accent, tongue and teeth,
But it's all in my head. Nobody *knows*
How Knox (or Shakespeare) spoke, just that they did,
And wrote. It's all a scholarly suppose
To think old writers sound the way they read.
Knox, though, the firebrand, rasping faith and Hell,
Clichéd the Presbyterian decibel
With pulpit rhetoric and prolix soul
Fueled by his brawny days pulling an oar,
Singing a Reformation barcarolle
As a French galley-slave, plotting his roar,
Scotland's future, and a Bibleless tongue –
Pulpit-delivered English, spoken, sung.
Blame? Who's to blame? Or what's to blame? Language
Lives by its own slowly unfolding rules

And chance morphologies, its shapes, and age,
Its histories the same as the people's.
Cut out our tongues to save the national face?
Let language happen in its commonplace,
Its ordinary, extraordinary
Occasions of speaking, singing, and writing,
Whether by C. M. Grieve or J. M. Barrie,
Excoriating, plain, or else delighting.
What happens in languages happens – it's
Destructive to contest their inner wits
Propelled by how time dips phonology
In what gets left behind by big events
Or weather, or how people work and play,
Their pleasures, sorrows and their discontents.
Pictish, Gaelic, Norse, Scots rural sounds, live
Even in altered voices, talkative
Survivals, fragments of noise, like place-names,
Those first poems in the crowded chronicle
Of the map of Scotland – a map proclaims
Languages' mix as ineradicable.
The onomastic mind looks into time,
Its one geography a named sublime.
    In our new Parliament, our accents mix
With confidence – get *that* into our lyrics!
No one's branded by a vocal stigma,
By mystical public schools or Oxbridge,
By England's creepy, sad, vocal enigma,
That patronising sound of patronage.
Now I hear children speak in a natural voice,
Accented zest and cadence. If it's choice
It's also nature. True to their time and place,
They show their mums and dads up, oldster frauds
Who buckled when their teachers set the pace
On how to speak (*'properly!'*), bawling the odds
Because we spoke the parish dialect,

Not junior BBC in our voice-wrecked
Pronunciation (so our teachers said).
Eagle, Hotspur, and *The Children's Newspaper,*
Wizard, Adventure, Daily Record, what I read
As a child made me no vocal leper nor
A local prig. I speak two ways, and write
In more than one, plural, and impolite.
    Live and let live. Promote the various.
Surrender to the spirit. Woodland. Moorland.
Put argument aside. Try to discuss.
Walk by the riverbank, and take your stand
By the midge-coloured water, the dark pools,
Rippling trout-rings. Watch the dozing owls.
That, too, is of our tongues, being our place,
Source of what strength we have, or character,
Wherever we came from or persisting trace
Of elsewhere lingering like a loyal spectre.
    Who legislates when Jock does something foul
To rolling consonantal R, or vowel,
Or lards his speech with epithets of F?
Well, we should. So, clean up your act. Turn down
The dreary, forthright volume, before we're deaf
From all that cursing from the angry town
And its intensifying Fs and Cs,
Indignant, crude monotonies!
    What's the language of laughter? Or sorrow
When it's suffered in silence? Or a love-moan,
A sob and cry in the night? Such sounds borrow
Each other's commonplace from polyphone
Humanity. They do not need a word.
Who cares whose fingers run across the keyboard?
'A note don't care who plays it,' a wise man said.
And only an indifferent poem gets lost
In its translation. In my flowerbed
Most plants and shrubs aren't native but have crossed

Seas, seasons, different climates, to be here
Thriving in shaded Scottish horticulture.
One day I'll feel the confidence to grow
Orchids. But let my lilies flourish in
This land and tongue of rain and cloud-shadow.
Lilies and roses, too, are of this nation.

MARGARET ELPHINSTONE

I'm standing on Trusty's Hill, an Iron Age hillfort in Kirkcudbrightshire with a commanding view of the Fleet estuary and valley. The Pictish symbol stone carved on the bedrock at the entrance suggests an alliance between the people who lived here, in the British kingdom of Rheged, and Picts from the distant north. Traces of Ogham script indicate connections with the Scots in Ireland. The fort was deliberately burnt to the ground in the seventh century. Recent excavations offer a glimpse into a world in which the Irish sea was a broad highway, where the borders of small kingdoms were fluid and uncertain, where conflict was endemic, and where trade routes extended as far as North Africa. One aspect of what is now Scotland remains unchanged: it is not, and never has been, peripheral or isolated. Since the ice retreated ten thousand years ago, the land has witnessed constant immigration and movement of peoples. There have always been long trade routes, wide-ranging political allegiances, religious shifts and cultural exchanges. There have also been tribal conflicts, civil wars and brutal invasions.

Perhaps because we live on an island, we in the currently united kingdom seem to have acquired very fixed ideas about boundaries. It's easy to forget just how debatable the lands on either side of the Tweed actually were for many centuries, how recently the northern and western islands owed allegiance elsewhere, or how semi-autonomous the Highlands were until 1746. When I was a child, I thought I could solve the dilemma of my divided origins if I lived in a house on the border with one half in England and one half in Scotland. I constructed an elaborate narrative built on that imaginary dwelling. Luckily it's not that simple; ambiguity means stimulation and flexibility.

When I first came to live in Scotland in 1970 I soon became aware of a limited, exclusive definition of nationhood that took me by surprise by excluding me (along, of course, with many others). My father's paternal family, though bearing a Scots name, had been in England for four generations. My mother was English/Jewish. My Musselburgh-born paternal grand-mother spoke with a limpid upper-class accent. I was born and educated in England, and I sound English. It took me years to realise that, ironically, given my circumstances at the time, issues of class as well as nationality were at stake, and that in the west of Scotland particularly I was a foreigner several times over. I learned when not to open my mouth. Alasdair Gray's pamphlet *Why Scots Should Rule Scotland* (1992) spoke of being 'Scottish by formation', which seemed to speak directly to my condition. Around the same time I encountered Benedict Anderson's *Imagined Communities*. Nationhood, I discovered, is necessarily indefinable, because every attempt at definition is a regressive reduction of all the people who regard themselves as rightfully dwelling in this place.

And yet our narrative of nationhood, as with citizens of every modern nation, is usually a process of looking back, apparently trying to recapture some lost state of static, homogenous, ingenuous identity. Today we can look back before 1603, or before 1707, to the once-upon-a-time when we had a resident monarch and our own single parliament. Indeed, as early as 1320 the Declaration of Arbroath, as David Daiches points out, purported to present the views of the Scottish nation, although the Scots were only one among many elements in a kingdom shaped by Britons, Gaels, Picts and Angles. The probable author of the Declaration, Abbot de Linton, was Anglo-Norman.

We're not the only country in Europe to have lost political and economic autonomy for long periods. The consequence seems to be a nostalgic longing for an imagined long-lost community, internally unified and hermetically sealed from the outside world. Although such nostalgia is a recurring feature of national narratives, a truly homogenous society untouched by external influences would be a disastrous cultural predicament. It's no accident that our greatest poets, writers, artists and musicians have operated in international forums, and derive their creative charge from internal contradictions.

Twice in my life I have voted for Scottish devolution in a referendum. I did this despite my terror of groups such as Scotwatch, a pressure group of the 1970s and 1980s who sought to drive outsiders (usually signifying the 'English') from Scotland. In May 1999 I cut Winnie Ewing's words out of the *Herald* and pinned them on the wall: *The Scottish Parliament, which adjourned on March 25, 1707, is hereby reconvened.* Looking back, I don't think my sense of elation at that time was misplaced. I fear some of my own ancestors may have been among the parcel of rogues in 1707. Or were they forward thinkers who saw the opportunities of English trade, English markets, access to a developing colonial empire and English prosperity at home? What would have happened to the Enlightenment if the Scots lords had not been bought and sold for English gold? And yet: *for as long as one hundred of us remain alive... Freedom is a noble thing; It makyth man to have lyking... A man's a man for a that...* In the jumble of well-rehearsed arguments and evocative quotations which fill my mind, I can only say that it seems to be the poetry that wins.

Poetry is perhaps one of the most powerful forces that human beings can command. As Fletcher of Saltoun famously expressed, *if a man were permitted to make all the ballads he need not care who should make the laws of a nation* (Letter to the Marquis of Montrose, 1703). Crude rhythms can persuade us to subscribe to crude ideas. But open-ended poetry offers a way to heighten awareness, and to change paradigms that seem in their own time to be irrevocably fixed. Never did we need a paradigm shift more than we do now. The title of Slavoj Žižek's book *Living in the End Times* succinctly states the situation I believe we face. Our world is finite, its resources running out, and we are incapable of stopping ourselves. Violence and religious divisions multiply. As ever, the poorest suffer most and the rich grow richer. Blame is useless; homo sapiens evolved mentally and emotionally equipped to deal with small-scale tribal survival, not with global catastrophe. Individuals struggle to address the appalling fact that we may be destroying the planet we live on. Denial takes many forms, from outright refusal to accept through to manic activism.

This is where politics – all politics – has failed us. The institutions of declining capitalism and vanished empire are the last places to look for radical alternatives with which to face the unimaginable future. Our government, along with that of every other western democracy, seems to be bogged down in the old familiar mantras of blame and dogma, and an obsession with detail at the expense of vision. Voters are cajoled by short-term promises, while the impetus to adapt to a changing world dissolves in futile arguments on policy.

Scotland is an imagined community, which exists in five million forms inside our heads. It can't be defined, but through the arts we construct alternative images of what we are, and what we could be. Because it's my imagined community, I can be effective here as I can be nowhere else. I know the place. I've chosen to live here all my adult life. I've experienced its geographical diversity, from Muckle Flugga to the Mull of Galloway. Most of my friends belong here, one way or another. There are certain places I literally know like the back of my hand. The most important events of my life have been shaped by this country where they happened. Scotland has made me the person that I am, and it has given me a voice, albeit an ambivalent one.

A nation of five million diverse individuals is small enough for individual voices to be heard. Many of us have observed, through causes dear to our hearts, how accessible our Scottish parliament is to petitions, lobbies and particular concerns. And yet, at the core of our own Parliament, we see reflected the massive failure of governments to address the most vital questions. Until we re-write the narrative 'Where do we come from? What are we? Where are we going?' we can't change anything. It's no accident that Gauguin wrote that aphorism on a painting of the same name, now in the Boston Museum of Fine Art. It is through art that we can question our story. The arts, as ever, could be the force that helps us to create new narratives: the stories we need to tell ourselves in order to cope with living in the end times.

It's ironic that we in Scotland have expended so much energy in debating where we have come from, and so little on where we are going. Words like 'freedom' and 'independence' signify nothing if we don't know what we need them for. Independence, for individuals and communities, can be empowering. It offers freedom, at the very least to make one's own mistakes. It takes away the escape route of moaning about how it's always somebody else's fault. I'm not sure that an independent Scotland will offer better solutions for living in the end times than any other community. But maybe it could give five million individuals the chance to make a better stab at it. Maybe we could take command of our outmoded institutions, and make them work for us instead of we for them. Maybe we could address the noxious inequalities of an increasingly inequitable society. Maybe we could rebuild a robust economy that resisted internal corruption, and took less advantage of other nations much poorer than ours. Maybe we could accept that the economy cannot grow for ever, and that capitalism is a fraud. Maybe we could learn to consume less, and share more. Maybe we could find ways to adapt to a changed environment so that our children can negotiate the war, famine and pestilence that follow from environmental, economic and civil collapse. Maybe we could... but only if we create visions of what we could be and how we could get there.

For all I know, two hundred years from now we'll be living in hill forts like Trusty's Hill, depending on a local warlord for protection against marauding bands mobilised by land hunger, civil unrest and blood feud. As I write that sentence, I'm haunted by Ralph Fiennes' recent film version of *Coriolanus*, set in a contemporary Bosnian-style dystopia. The context is modern, but the violent society portrayed has occurred repeatedly throughout human history, as Shakespeare understood very well: a familiar scenario as empires collapse.

1500 years ago the community on Trusty's Hill gained vision and some resilience from the diverse skills and cultures that formed it. It grew, people lived their lives there, and then it disappeared into the dark. Further into the future, when humans have gone, Scotland will once again be a burning desert, or another ice sheet. The environment of the more immediate future will certainly be the result of human interventions. We can't stop change, because change is the condition under which we live.

I think we can best prepare for it by constructing a community which works. It needs to be small enough for individuals to have a voice, because individuals are more radical and flexible than the engines of politics and economics. Only individuals can collectively re-shape their shared narratives. Our nation needs to have a realistic sense of itself, of its diversity and differences, because otherwise people will end up blaming and fighting each other. It needs to adapt to times that are going to be more different from the world we have known than we have yet dreamed of. It needs to uphold human rights and freedoms, including the freedom to imagine a world that could be better and fairer than the one we inhabit. It needs to love the land it lives on, otherwise it will destroy the ground that sustains it. It needs to know itself, which means being honest, and being ready to listen to all its different voices. And I think it needs to be psychologically independent, or it won't be able do anything for itself at all.

LEIGH FRENCH AND GORDON ASHER

'The interests of the oppressors lie in changing the consciousness of the oppressed not the situation which oppresses them.'

> Paulo Freire, *Pedagogy of the Oppressed* (1968)

Much of leftist debate on 'the Scottish question' is perplexing, not to say frustrating. What could be an opportunity for dialogue is instead functioning as a process of closure, where independence is posited as *ipso facto* 'progressive' – as if, in Gerry Hassan's words, 'independence (give or take all the known variables) is a known quality'.[1] Such thinking serves to elide and co-opt struggles for social justice in ways that demand critical attention. This essay aims to open up a critical dialogue on independence, self-determination and nation-building, and to re-focus these questions on *participation* as empowerment.

Our notion of social justice encompasses both a politics of redistribution and a politics of recognition; an approach oriented to 'changing both the economic structure and the status order of society'.[2] Recognising the integrated nature of the injustices of contemporary society – also between societies – we propose a strategy of *participatory change* which exposes and addresses *intersectional* oppressions: how biological, social and cultural categories such as gender, race, ability, class (its status component), etc., interact on multiple, often simultaneous levels with capitalist economic relations to contribute to systemic inequality.

Rather than taking a pro- or an anti-stance to voting (if at all) in the referendum, here we seek to problematise the central terms, narratives, limits, assumptions and promises of the independence campaigns, in a spirit of critical dialogue. An abiding concern is the importance of wider contexts, influences and consequences; we cannot separate the assumed 'interest-bearing unit' of Scotland from its global socio-economic contexts.

In attempting to move beyond any simplistic yes/no approach, we ask:

> What is meant by independence, by whom, and what kind of society would an 'independent' Scotland be likely to produce?

> How might people work towards social justice through these debates/communicative processes – if indeed it is possible within a nation-state framework intimately and comfortably tied to capitalism?

> What of the (progressives') appeal to notions of nationalism incorporating claims of 'self-determination' and social democracy?

Much independence rhetoric across the 'Yes' campaign(s) is superficial and internally contradictory – insisting that 'Scots' should vote yes whatever our competing conceptions of a desirable future society. 'Independence' here functions as a utopian category into which people pour their desires, hopes and aspirations – such as for freedom, equality and democracy. This condition is to be achieved, it seems, not through struggle but passive support for hierarchical campaigns derivative of parliamentarians and electoral strategists. Deferring to 'experts' only entrenches the alienation of people's own capacity to effect transformation, affirming the empty paradigm of capitalist / nation-state / representative 'democracy'. This pattern guarantees that 'post-independence' power, wealth and resources will continue to be determined by capitalist relations, and the perpetuation of systemic oppressions.

I. 'Democracy'

Representation is a mythical form of 'democracy'. It is neither representative of (or accountable to) those whom it claims to be, nor is it democratic; in that it does not lead to the people of a given state being the decision makers – to people having the ultimate power over policies to the extent that they are affected by them. Rather, it tends towards hierarchical, authoritarian, centralised rule through a set of institutions, systems and relations – electoral systems, political parties, constitutional structures and powers, limits on political 'debate', voice and participation etc.

Further, it is vital to recognise that 'representative democracies' are set within (and indeed serve to maintain and evolve) much wider formal and informal, internal and external networks and structures of institutional and relational power that serve to further foreclose notions of legitimacy, accountability and participation.

Even within this 'representative' paradigm, Scotland has yet to attain 'normative' levels of European democracy: 'At the local level Scotland is the least democratic country in Europe. The state of local democracy in Scotland means that it is virtually impossible for any community to make any decision about itself'.[3] Debates around a sovereign parliament for Scotland also tend to neglect the contemporary culture of intense corporate lobbying at Holyrood. Critical oversight for informing such debate has been further foreclosed by the increasing neoliberalisation of the Scottish education system. Alongside corporate media influence, this has led not merely to the curtailment of holding power to account but exemplifies how corporate power is accomplished through integration into governance.

The referendum, we are told, is precisely about Scotland choosing its own future. But the SNP's vision of independence accepts in advance the neo-liberal *doxa* of competition, markets and growth. It seems important to emphasise that *referenda* are not liberating acts of direct democracy. Capitalism isn't actually being threatened here; in truth, it seems many left-nationalists only dare to hope that a truly 'Scottish' capitalist society would be more generously welfarist. Campaigning merely for a 'Yes' vote at the referendum arguably displaces and forestalls current popular struggle for transformation against current very real threats, onto an underdetermined yet supposedly more promising future territory.

The consensus around 'competitive nationalism' (where aspects of life and identity, including education, arts, sports and culture, are harnessed as marks of distinction; as competitive factors of national economic advantage) underscores the cosmetic nature of the social-democratic reforms supposedly in prospect, just as much as the continuity-exploitation of oil and imperative of infinite growth on a finite planet. Progressives' appeals to the doctrine of 'self-determination' only endorse a state-foundational individualism whereby the presumed free will of the individual and that of the people are conflated; as a 'collective individual' possessing its own sovereign free will, 'we' are socially realised through the single discourse of the nation. Such appeals to 'self-determination' legitimise preconceived claims by the 'self-appointed' political elite that to 'act under the assumption that their own sovereign free wills can not but be identical with sovereign free will of the people and therefore with sovereign free will of the individual'.[4]

Actual self-determination concerns individual and collective autonomy as articulated through *participatory democratic* decision-making – the difficult process of changing what the reproduction of life means in both pragmatic and phantasmatic terms – none of which is conspicuous in the campaigns thus far. We argue that political, economic and social transformation has to be communicated, contested, struggled for – transformation is not inherent to 'independence', and will certainly not be achieved simply by campaigning for a 'Yes' vote.

II. 'Cultural Intimacy'

A 'national citizenry' is not a fixed, static, coherent and indivisible entity but composed of different people with different positions and interests, with the state's functionaries also reflecting internal divisions of composition. Michael Herzfeld's notion of 'cultural intimacy' refers to the often contradictory ways in which state and local practices interact in creating and institutionalising national imagery and sentiment in the construction of nation-state formations – the processes of the organisation of territory (national boundaries), ethnos, and government apparatus.[5]

The appeal to nationalism involved in the construction of a nostalgic and mythical, homogenous 'Britishness' – be it Royal Weddings, the Jubilee or 2012 Olympics, to be sold at home and abroad, and wielded as a disciplinary and marketing tool for the manufacture, maintenance and evolution of consent – is replaced by a terribly similar 'Scottishness'. As such, it's a sterile nationalism, remaining firmly within the dialectic of coloniser-colonised, portrayed as a wish 'to throw off imperialist rule in order to assert already established national identity, whose only flaw is to have been contaminated and repressed by the presence of the colonialists'.[6] It hardly needs spelling out that this mirage denies both local and global realities.

III. Geographical Communities

Focusing on nationalism – on national/ethnic identity – homogenises and flattens our multiple, complex and mutable identities thus masking oppressions, repressions and exploitations centred on them – as these axes of identity interact on multiple and often simultaneous levels, contributing to systematic social inequality. Surely this is dangerous territory indeed for those of us focusing on social justice? This flattened discourse on oppressions has a strange, strangled way of representing 'power'; always just out of view, as if the political class and its interests were merely 'geographically' bound, and spatial proximity was the real concern. The SNP have clearly decided that a spatialised discourse is more palatable than more divisive alternatives; thus independence is about bringing power 'home', and ensuring decisions concerning Scotland are taken 'in' Scotland. This spatial cleaving sets up a disingenuous 'location' of the interests of the co-ordinator/political class – and so locationally legitimises them closer to home as the 'solver' of the internal effects of now 'external' problems. This model seems fundamentally anti-political, ushering in a *post-politics* for post-independence Scotland. Erik Swyngedouw characterises 'the post-political condition [as] one in which consensus has been built around the inevitability of neo-liberal capitalism as an economic system' – that is, 'a political formation that actually forecloses the political'.[7] Swyngedouw insists 'that this post-political condition in fact annuls democracy', as we are presently seeing in Ireland, Italy and Greece. What are the prospects for post-independence 'independence', understood in these terms? An exercise in managing conceptions of governance – claiming consensual participation and community democracy for a process that merely delivers to neoliberalism a public neutered by its 'liberation' into the same old 'end of history'?

Having the political class closer to home doesn't necessarily make replacing them any easier, never mind challenging the idea of a political class *per se*.[8] If anything, the intensification of the nationalist-centred independence project championed by much apparently 'progressive' opinion could have a significant effect in mystifying power and oppressive relations and undermining self-organisation through their replacement by a passive support for 'the nation'.

Who is offering actual alternatives to the *disaster capitalism* of continued and entrenched 'austerity' – in reality, the rapid-fire, corporate-state re-engineering of societies reeling from shock?

IV. Incidental heirs?

Nation states are not *natural* but historically contingent, ongoing political constructs, reflective of power struggles of empire and colonialism. 'Scots' have been foot-soldiers, leaders and beneficiaries of empire and neo-colonialism – not just historically, but in the present. Scotland's institutions, systems of law and governance, its pursuance of economics and politics, sit within that, not aside separate from it, but as fundamental functioning, reproductive participants in it. Scotland is not simply some colonially-tainted otherwise-bastion-of-virtue that can be removed from the history upon which where we are today is contingent. Scotland participated in, and reproduced, modes of oppression many nationalists would like to externalise as 'alien' to claimed core national social democratic values, the remedy to which figures independence as mystical 'release'.

Where does this leave hopes for participatory democracy? The 'civic' dimension of the SNP's nationalism is an ideology of social partnership predicated on the managed appearance of public participation. It is about delivering people to policy – to the imperatives of neoliberal capitalism. If independence is 'achieved' on these terms we will merely have replaced one set of post-democratic political governors / managers with another.

Moreover, if 'Scotland' remains as fully within and reproducing international capital relations, to what extent can it be 'sovereign' (within the realities of a nexus of powerful governments, institutions and financial interests: US, EU, NATO, UN,

IMF, World Bank, WTO)? We are therefore left asking if it's at all possible to seek transformation for social justice through voting for independence if any campaigning for any new nation state is *ipso facto* nation building?

A more meaningful vision of independence would not be about converting alleged cultural shame or inferiority into pride; following Lauren Berlant, it would require 'a hard confrontation with and a very difficult process of changing what the reproduction of life means in both pragmatic and phantasmatic terms'.[9]

Beyond State and Capital?

What roles, if any, can exist for notions of independence/national self-determination? If such roles are possible (thereby raising transitionary issues), can a conception of independence for a Scotland provide a useful opportunity in struggles for social justice? Further, if it can be, is it at present? And if not, how could it be?

How can a process for and beyond independence take an anti-imperialist/anti(neo)colonialist stance – one that acknowledges the realities of historic and contemporary projects of empire and neo-colonialism? One that is also necessarily anti-capitalist/anti-corporate? For the oppressions that both produce (throughout, across, between societies) are intertwined. As post-Soviet 'new' states exemplify, multinational interests can also thrive on smaller 'centralised' interdependent states.

Must such stances lead to a position, in the here and now, that rejects states and nations or do/can/should such stances accept the tactical or strategic necessity/desirability of transitional arrangements (perhaps even viewed as necessarily pre-conditional) that encompass the (re)creation of nation states?

How, if at all, do such considerations play out with regard to actual and potential moves towards independence for Scotland? If social justice is the vision, what strategies and tactics, based in our contemporary contextual realities, can get us from here to there?

What we perceive in much of the contemporary framing of this debate is a division appearing between state-building (the political classes and the continuity of their privileges/interests) and securing a referendum 'win' through identitarian myth building. What is to be the relationship between the state and society? Who is to decide? How? – and if not in the 'doing' then when?

It would be pointless 'breaking' the British state only for it to come back in multiple forms of itself, replicating the self-same interests/powers/ privileges. So it's not just a case of voting to dismantle a British state structure, while leaving concurrent interests intact, but of politicising the processes and realising the participatory potentials of *actually* disassembling state power. Taking an active role, as agents in these processes, cannot be postponed out of perceived/projected 'fragility' in the present, nor in the name of 'unity'. Independence is not a moment to vote for, but a process of state formation to participate in (or be excluded from) or to resist.

Our concern with the 'Yes' campaigns' consensualism ('optimism', 'confidence', and forced positivity generally), and significant sections of progressive positionality, is the consequences (intended or otherwise) of their proposals; if they were successful, they should leave us in, *with*, and *for* the nexus of capitalism/nation-state/representative 'democracy'.

Our proposal is for a clearer orientation of not just 'against', but 'beyond' – speaking to a society and world that is post-both capitalism and nation state (a dissolving rather than a devolving of the state – which may include independence). A proposal for collective grass-roots empowerment, of praxis for social justice, that include dialogues of engagement with the issues of independence, nationalism and self-determination allowing for the divergences and possible futures on the way. Processes that continue whatever the results of the referendum. These debates need to be about *being* and *becoming*, rather than accepting a flattening assertion of who 'we' are as premised on a mythical, 'natural', homogenised and non-conflicted past and promised future. It is not about envisaging/imagining a better capitalism – though non-reformist reforms will be essential to achieving transformational change – it is about working towards a post-capitalist society. It is about other, better, worlds that are possible, necessary and under construction.

(We would like to additionally acknowledge the influence of the ideas and writings of: Naomi Klein, Michael Albert, Stephen Brookfield, Noam Chomsky, *Glasgow Anarchists*, *Common Sense* journal and John Holloway, and everyone else unreferenced in our brevity.)

Notes

[1] 'We need to have a One Question Referendum. It is that simple!', 28 January 2012, www.gerryhassan.com/uncategorized/we-need-to-have-a-one-question-referendum-it-is-that-simple/

[2] Nancy Fraser, 'Social Justice in the Age of Identity Politics: Redistribution, Recognition, and Participation', in Nancy Fraser and Axel Honneth, *Redistribution or Recognition: A Political-Philosophical Exchange* (London: Verso, 2003), p. 22.

[3] 'The Silent Crisis: Failure and Revival in Local Democracy in Scotland', The Jimmy Reid Foundation, April 2012, http://reidfoundation.org/portfolio/the-silent-crisis-failure-and-revival-in-local-democracy-in-scotland/

[4] Zlatko Hadžidedić, 'Nationalism and Liberalism: The Paradoxes of Self-Determination', 23 July 2010, www.ifimes.org/default.cfm?Jezik=En&Kat=10&ID=544

5   Michael Herzfeld, *Cultural Intimacy: Social Poetics in the Nation-State* (London: Routledge, 1997).

6   Terry Eagleton, 'Foreword' to Kristin Ross, *The Emergence of Social Space: Rimbaud and the Paris Commune* (Minneapolis, MN: University of Minnesota Press, 1989), p. viii.

7   Erik Swyngedouw, 'The Antinomies of the Postpolitical City: In Search of a Democratic Politics of Environmental Production', *International Journal of Urban and Regional Research* 33.3 (September 2009) 601–20; www.scribd.com/doc/56913989/The-Antinomies-of-the-Postpolitical-City-In-Search-of-a-Democratic-Politics-ofEnvironmental-Production

8   Glasgow AF member, 'Independent and free? A Glasgow anarchist's take on Scottish independence', http://libcom.org/library/independent-free-glasgow-anarchists-take-scottish-independence

9   Gesa Helms, Marina Vishmidt and Lauren Berlant, 'Affect & the Politics of Austerity: An interview exchange with Lauren Berlant', *Variant* 39/40 (Winter 2010); www.variant.org.uk/39_40texts/berlant39_40.html

A longer version of this text is available at: http://groundleft.wordpress.com/2012/08/27/crises-capitalism-and-independence-doctrines.

JANICE GALLOWAY

Who do you think you are? The phrase that clanged like an iron bar through my childhood is still waking me up at night, wondering if it's overstepping the mark to conjecture seriously who I think should run the country I live and work in. You're not entitled to an opinion, you're entitled to shut up, my sister's consistent reminder of my own smallness in the world, gets in the way. Are the Scots entitled to have thoughts as big as how we wish to be governed? Can we be trusted to make such a decision sensibly, or can we decide only in the throes of tartan-coated, sentimental, pseudo-patriotic huff because that's what we're like? The word chippy springs to mind: me, Andy Murray, the whole bloody lot of us may well be too chippy to be trusted with David Hume-style rationalism.

Well, are we? Is this country lock and stock so far away from the true seat of political reality of those in the know, that we are incapable of grasping what is at stake? I'd go so far as to contend that most of us, by which I mean most of us who ever wonder what Scottish means at all, are confused by the separate responses of heart, head, gut and memory on the subject of secession. In the USA, we're 'cute' – or at least our accents are. In Scandinavia, Ireland, Wales and Canada, we pass for long-lost cousins, colourful Celts or probable allies of another country in bed with an elephant. In South Africa, we are colonisers who were colonised, in France, Jacobins pining for a Romantic King over the water, and in Russia, we are expected to know our Robert Burns. I am exaggerating slightly, but not outrageously.

Certainly, in beautiful and bountiful England, the most frequent response to my voice is that I am Not English. There usually follows some banter recalling Boswell and Dr Johnson (Boswell: 'Mr. Johnson, I do indeed come from Scotland, but I cannot help it.' Johnson: 'That, I find, is what a very great many of your countrymen cannot help') or some other light-hearted acknowledgement of the attitudinal history between our two countries. In less formal first encounters, the remarks can be more open and more heart-felt.

1. London: me and a writer from Oban, sharing a cab to Westminster. The cabbie notices my hair colour and my friend's Highland jaw in the rear-view mirror. He checks several times, especially when we laugh. The Bank of Scotland tenner we offer as a fare, however, goes too far. No use, he says. It's Scotch. We have nothing else. He won't touch it. The money, he explains slowly, is Scotch. My friend shrugs. Look, he says, it's all we have. Stop buggering about and take it. The cabbie not only casts the offending note to the wind, but tells us to fuck off and, as we walk off, sprays the now empty passenger seats with a hissing lavender fug of air-freshener for good measure. 'Bleedin Scotch', he mutters. 'Smart-mouth bleedin bastard Scotch'.

2. Shrewsbury M&S, shopping. A stranger approaches politely and asks if I'd read the cooking instructions off a ready-meal since he's forgotten his glasses and I do. You're from Scotland, he says. I am indeed. Ooh, he says. We used to go to Scotland a lot for holidays. You don't get that voice round here very often! Apparently delighted, he shows off a picture of his wife in a wheelchair at Loch Ness. It's a braw brikt moonlikt nikt the noo, he says. I love Scotch people. He embraces me. Tight.

Deep down, sometimes surprisingly deep down, English feelings about North Britain run deep. For the most part, these feelings have little to do with real Scots, but notions of generalised antipathy or affection inspired by whatever we represent to the viewer at the time. I was mildly surprised and not surprised, therefore, by a recent poll that suggested that for the most part the English want the Union to continue, but, as John Curtice of Strathclyde University remarked, 'they probably would not die in a ditch to keep it preserved. After all, for most people in England, Scotland is not a significant other'.

But from the Scottish side of the Union – for which marital analogies are inescapable – a creeping estrangement can no longer be ignored. Now, there's a half-filled suitcase in the hall and a flurry of panic. Less than a third of the Scottish electorate want full independence, we're told, but they fancy the sound of so-called Devo-Max – which sounds like the right to an own front and back door key in an adjacent flat. The popularity of the Devo-Max option, somewhat resented as a kind of cheating by Westminster, tells us something we already know: unexpect-edly strong feelings and resentments are always part of the emotional reckoning that is separation. This much, for the time being, is clear.

When the *Guardian* asked if I'd write a little on what being Scottish and/or British meant to me, however, I was ill-prepared for the trepidation that kept me awake at night, tormented that anything I thought could be expressed clearly at all. Perhaps the question struck too personal a nerve. So I sidestepped the Scottishness of the issue and opted for the British half of things as less equivocal. Being British, to me at least, means and has always meant I live on the landmass Britannia, those islands the Romans saw as three natural parts: Caledonia, Hibernia, Albion. I love the variety of our landscape and wildlife and its myths and histories – full of treachery and deals concocted by the powerful few over the heads of their respective peoples – are tales to which I feel entitled. From the Border Ballads to Blake and far beyond, I love the mongrel English language and its sometimes flagrant, sometimes veiled roots of our words and common phrases. I love the range of accents and dialects in which it dresses itself, the half-dialects of former foreigners come to live here, of new English-speakers who adapt the local accent of the region in which they settle and make it new. I love hearing Welsh and Gaelic though I can't understand a word of either, because they are alive and sound like music, and I love the sheer orneriness of our Latin-inflected grammars. Now that RP (the accent one tends to buy at public school) and what it tried so hard to signify is less of a big deal, even the accent that likes to insist it is not an accent is enjoyable. I work with words – why would I not enjoy this rich variety while being completely capable of separating the class signifiers impressed upon them? I can and I do. I dislike racial stereotyping largely because it is tired and not funny. But I like these islands. Every so often, I feel I belong.

This sense of belonging has nothing to do with fiscal or governmental union and everything to do with proximity, amity and variance. These things together seem to me to throw up a proper respect for difference. It never occurs to me that Scotland and England are one, any more than it occurs to me that Scotland and Wales are one or that Monaco is not France. The Thistle and the Rose (both prickly) have different political make-ups. Our cultures have different histories, our languages different influences: our creative wellsprings and aspirations are often different too. All this shows in the way we use words, inflect their meanings and express our keenest hopes for the society we'd like to help create. Most often, we have expressed those hopes only to ourselves in Scottish variants of British parties, the main power-base of which is in the south. In the Central Belt, we trusted the Labour party to deliver at least a vague interest in social justice, while the Highlands and Borders placed some faith in Liberalism and Edinburgh kept the odd Tory in office. Now all is changed, changed utterly. A terrible beauty is on the slouch.

That Scottish votes over the years have seldom delivered a matching government is only part of what changed. Certainly, the awful nineties 'greed is good' years when the North in general became the Conservative Party's petri dish were a caustic reminder of our increasing inconsequentiality to just about any Westminster-based party. The SNP – once seen by many as clannish, MacDiarmid-obsessed or even arcane – began to look like a serious alternative. The SNP, in response, seemed to re-organise itself as a party engaged with those Scottish priorities that Westminster parties found increasingly old-hat, too out of touch with modern business thinking or just not very important. The SNP (Mr Salmond in particular) has become good at a fair number of Scottish priorities while Labour has more and more resembled a whale beached and abandoned by its former kind and the Liberals – well, it seems likely that party's new reputation for breaking promises in return for short-term power will be a long time casting off. Even when you see it coming, it is undeniable that disenchantment hurts. Nonetheless, we will move forward because it is the only thing to be done. We will take stock, reassess, think afresh. One of the things to think afresh about is whether, after thirty years of being sidelined, the Scottish electorate matters tuppence to the mainstream parties, or whether, given the go-getting, winner-takes-all priorities of today's New Realist politicians, we are, frankly, too small and too far away to be worth bothering about. Should we hope for a change of present bullish marketing-techniques-honed political culture, or find some change within ourselves – the wait-and-see or actively-choose choice we know from our more intimate relationships writ large.

One thing I am completely sure of is that people need a measure of governance over the territory upon which they stand. Just as a child's sense of worth is bound up in his or her opinions being taken seriously by those they look to as guardians, an adult's – a whole country's – works much the same way. Self-esteem makes for confident kids, confident teens, a confident people. If Scottish self-esteem – a phrase that makes one psychoanalyst I know reach for the term 'oxymoron' – is reflected in the self-care racked up by our national statistics for liver disease, dental problems, drug-addiction, poor diet, male suicide and routine domestic abuse linked to football games, we are not a people overburdened with amour-propre.

I do not wish to conflate class with nationality. The working classes of England, Wales and Northern Ireland can hardly feel valued as pay-gaps widen beyond belief, bankers make their own greed-driven laws with impunity, available jobs decrease and our children prepare for a life with little or no chance of social mobility. But I believe the preferred solutions to improve health, education, welfare, legal and political change may be significantly different, which is to say political choice may well be as much a product of blood and land as our distinct land-scapes. The restoration of the Scottish and Welsh Parliaments has already shown that some policies (think student fees, prescription charges, costs of care for the elderly) already reflect such differences, many of them to the general disgruntlement of the English people. This is healthy. This is democratic. Thinking about politics has to be better than placing the burden for our national self-esteem on sportsmen. In order to build a future based on hope rather than fatalism or loss of nerve, we need to remind ourselves we matter by making such decisions gently, regularly, like medicine till we are confident enough to dare to think for ourselves.

Meanwhile, I observe that no couple considering break-up ever got Better Together without consultation, discussion, a few honest truths. And while the SNP have a cool and erudite political mind in Alex Salmond, they still need to press home a motivation more akin to Small is Beautiful than Scotland the Brave if they are to reassure the broadest cross-section of a tradi-tionally cautious, slow to trust, often self-punishing people. They will also need to address their heedless lack of a powerful arts policy – for to foster the vision and voices of our contem-porary arts is to foster necessary self-awareness, self-trust and hope in the power of thought so necessary to a sound sense of self-worth and thus to political change. Certainly, for the SNP, or any other party claiming to have the interests of the Scottish people at heart, to continue to ignore the 'half-baked, hollowed-out, public-sector version of market theory' that is Creative Scotland would be criminal neglect of the most basic element of good government – to ensure the people's hopes and dreams for what can be. (See Joyce MacMillan's skewering of Creative Scotland in *The Scotsman*, 25 May 2012.)

Awkward questions are a sign of independent and well-tended minds. What most would encourage a culture with a moral rather than a monetary core? What most seeks to take account of the quality of our air, our farmland, the lives of our livestock? What would help our industries not only survive but be competitive, innovative and small-scale sustainable again? Allow our engineers, designers and manufacturers to make things not based on quick sales, sudden obsolescence and land-fill? What would let our thinkers, scientists and artists flourish and inspire a whole nation with the excellence of what they do? These questions are not interested in fear: they are interested in the future. And that is why they matter.

Whatever we choose, I hope we do it hopefully, confidently, sure our country and people are valuable. Do not be afraid that England will miss us, for we will still be there, on exactly the same landmass we have always occupied. All we have to lose is what we signified – a jumble of mean-minded stereotypes, our lost regiments and regimental glories, our status as the last kick of Empire, our sense we somehow deserve not only less than we hope for, but a smack for getting big ideas in the first place.

How much would we like to define ourselves? To take a leap of faith?

Let's make it a lot.

MAGI GIBSON

We all know one.

The woman who stays in a marriage with a husband she doesn't love or respect. In fact, she doesn't even like him. And we all wonder why she doesn't leave. Not least because she moans about him constantly; how he over-rules her, even as he insists that her opinion counts. How he belittles her, but oh-so-affectionately; can't she take a bit of gentle ribbing? How he says they're in a marriage of equals, but as he's the bigger earner it's only natural he gets a bigger say in how they live, what they spend their money on. (And anyway, why would she want to worry herself with those things when he can take care of them for her?)

We look at this woman. She has all the trappings of someone who's doing well; stylish haircut, fashionable clothes, gold jewellery. She has her own car, a couple of credit cards, two foreign holidays a year. But the outer trappings count for nothing. Underneath she is stunted. Like a plant growing in the wrong conditions. You go out for drinks with her some-times. After the third drink she reminisces about what she was like before; bright, intelligent, independent-minded. She had potential. She had dreams. After the fourth drink she becomes animated about what she could have – should have – been.

Everything this woman says and does reveals one thing. One thing that over-rides all her superficial affluence: her spouse's control over how she lives affects her sense of self-worth, and threatens to subsume her very identity. (Of course, from time to time, he allows her little victories. He likes having a 'kept' wife. It feeds his sense of being a Big Man.)

As time goes on she mythologises her past more and more, and develops a self-indulgent bitterness as she gripes about how everything that goes wrong is HIS fault.

You look at her with some sadness. You see what she cannot. No matter how materially comfortable her life is, as long as she stays in this union of unequals, she will never realise her own unique potential.

So why doesn't she leave?

FEAR.

Fear of what? Of failure? Of taking full responsibility for herself? Of being the architect of her own future? Of not having someone else to blame when things go wrong?

To be fair, this fear has not grown and developed totally by chance. It's the result of years and years of being told (mostly by him, and he can be very persuasive) that she's not strong enough to cope on her own. In 'Harlot Red', a short story I wrote at the time of devolution, the woman tells her partner she's being stifled by their relationship, she needs to leave. As she stands in the doorway with her packed suitcases, he says:

> 'You can't be serious. You'll be back in a fortnight. You'll not be happy on your own. Who's going to look after the bills? Who's going to fix the heating if it breaks down? Who's going to get up in the middle of the night if you hear a strange noise? You're fooling yourself. You need me.'

Does he really believe she needs him? Or is he psychologically manipulating her so that she is too scared to go it alone? How many women have had these words said to them over the years?

In the classic feminist short story 'The Yellow Wallpaper', written by Charlotte Perkins Gilman more than a century ago, the husband – a physician in this case, presented not as a misogynistic monster, but as a caring and moral man – diagnoses his wife with mental illness when she wants to grow and develop by writing and painting. He needs her to stay as she is, dependent and weakened, so that his control of her, necessary to his sense of being dominant, is not threatened.

So what has all this to do with Scotland?

It might seem strange to anthropormophise a country so often symbolised by whisky-swilling, pugnacious, football-playing, hairy, head-butting hardmen as a woman – and a weak woman at that. But is that what the once fierce and feisty Scotland is turning into? A scared, wee, moanin-faced woman trapped in an unequal marriage. (What's more, a polygamous marriage. Scotland is just one of England's wee wives.)

No wonder the bell-ringer at St Giles Cathedral reputedly played *Why am I so sad on this my wedding day*, and civil unrest broke out in many parts of Scotland when the Act of Union was signed. Right from that first wedding night Scotland was never going to be an equal partner. It could even be claimed it was a forced marriage; by all accounts it was not the choice of the people. It was certainly a marriage of financial convenience – if not necessity – and yes, Scotland may well have benefitted in some ways over the past three centuries. But perhaps it's time for Scotland to get off her knees, stop snivelling, and prove that she's got the balls to determine her own future – like the lineage of feisty Scotswomen I hail from, who would have lived on bread and water before they'd compromise their beliefs or kow-tow to anyone.

For amazingly, even three centuries of grudging subordination and barely disguised colonisation have not eradicated Scotland's sense that she *does* have her own distinct identity. As a child I was never in any doubt that *I* was Scottish. Oh, I was told that I was British too, but that never spoke to my heart. But my Scottishness? That flowed through my veins as strongly as the bagpipe music my father occasionally played on winter nights.

In our wonderful, wee council house, I was taught to be proud of Scottish education. I attended one of the first comprehensive schools in the country. I learned that to be Scottish meant to be part of a co-operative, caring community; to have a socialist mindset where hard work with either your hands or your brain was honorable and should be rewarded with decent wages; that everyone should have free healthcare and decent living conditions; that tolerance and acceptance of difference was a good thing. I loved the lyrics of the Burns song 'A Man's A Man For A' That', and (despite being a girl) thought it was speaking directly to me and epitomised the best of what being Scottish meant.

But that is *my* sense of Scottishness. What is happening to our collective sense of Scottishness now, in the twenty-first century?

Like that woman we both know, does today's Scotland spend too much time harking back to an unfulfilled past, rather than planning for a fulfilled future? A Scotland that loves nothing more than greetin into its whisky glass about how it hates the bastard English? Is that the Scotland we have today? A nation happy to package up and sell its sense of self in couthy tartan shortbread tins and tartan tammies and faux-fur sporrans? To peddle a plastic-heather-kitsch-and-keech culture while its young people develop an alarming sense of victimhood, and despite (apparently) better education than ever before, confuse nationalism – with all its negative connotations of nasty and nazi – with national pride?

If we want to be treated as a nation inside or outside the union our sense of who we collectively are has to be more than a snazzy collection of designer kilts; an absentee, misogynistic film star; and a horde of Saltire-draped, ginger-wigged football fans famous for being good-natured losers.

Scotland will continue to have a crisis of identity until she stands on her own two feet and faces down the demons – many of them imaginary as demons so often are – stationed between her and her future. A future which could offer so much; not least self-respect; the opportunity to close the ever-widening gap between rich and poor; and a true democracy unfettered by inherited privilege and archaic undemocratic structures.

But will twenty-first century Scotland have the guts?

Remember that unfulfilled woman we all know? One day you get fed up with her constant moaning about her husband, so you challenge her. 'Why don't you leave him?' you ask. 'Strike out on your own. Be who *you* want to be.'

She stares into the bottom of her whisky glass as if she might find the answer there.

> 'It's complicated,' she sighs. 'We've been together a long time. I wouldn't know where to start.'
> 'It's not that complicated,' you answer. 'Scientists decoded the human genome. Now that was complicated.'
> 'I might end up with less than I've got now,' she mutters.
> 'There are different ways of having less,' you say.
> She doesn't answer. Just goes up to the bar and orders more drinks. 'Make mine a double,' she says to the barman.

Then there was the woman in my story. She left despite her partner's infantilisation of her and his fear-mongering. She's her own woman now, and a dab-hand at fixing the heating. Her husband, meanwhile, has been set free to forge a new and different sense of self too.

And the woman in 'The Yellow Wallpaper'? Unable to grow and develop her creativity in a positive way, she descends into madness, her unused energies turning inwards. Soon she loses all sense of who she is and spends her days crawling round the attic room, a pitiful, twisted version of the woman she could have been.

Of course, 'Harlot Red' is a contemporary story. 'The Yellow Wallpaper' was written over a century ago. Women – and nations, even small ones – have much more ability to be independent these days. If that's what they really want.

ALASDAIR GRAY

Settlers and Colonists

A Scottish wordsmith said, 'Outgoers and incomers made, make every land'. Yes. Both kinds can be divided into Settlers or Colonists. The Irish tribes who brought Christianity to what we now call Argyllshire and gave Scotland its name were incoming settlers. So were the Anglo-Saxon invaders who gave England its name, though for a while King Canute regarded England as a province of his Danish empire – a province rather than a colony, because the Danish settlers who supported him were mingling well with what were now Anglo-Saxon natives. For centuries Norwegian kings regarded Iceland, Orkney and Shetland as provinces of their empire, but had to treat the Western Isles and Sutherland as colonies before natives there, helped by Scots kings, won free of them. The Dutch empire for a while contended on three continents with the British empire, but in Malaysia English colonists supported by their Royal Navy soon ousted the Dutch, and in America (despite old New York being once New Amsterdam) Dutch settlers were overwhelmed by those from England, though together both European incomers expelled American natives. Only South Africa had enough Dutch settlers to dominate the native majority, and survive the Dutch empire's extinction, and after stout resistance become a British empire protectorate on their own terms.

Colonists and settlers may start with the same homeland and some loyalty to it, a loyalty dependent on support the homeland gives them. The difference between these two sorts of invader becomes obvious when they have subdued the local natives by exterminating many of them, as in Australia, driving them away, as in North America, enslaving them as in South America, or (more rarely) giving some of them equal rights, as may be the case in New Zealand. As soon as incoming settlers in these lands no longer needed the government, army or navy of their homelands they were on the way to self-government. But for roughly two centuries most subjects of the British empire were ruled by native Britons employed directly by the London government. They were colonists, not settlers. They regarded marriage between themselves and the local natives as almost unthinkable, calling it *going native*. Hardly any thought of uniting with those they ruled. If successful in one part of the empire they could be sent to work for it in another before finally retiring to the land of their birth, where some even took part in its government. The Duke of Wellington, a successful Irish general in the Indian army, was sent to fight Napoleon's empire in Europe and afterward had a spell as Britain's Prime Minister.

The USA has made all such imperialism a thing of the past. It does not exploit foreign lands by planting settlers in them, as Britain did in Canada and Australia, or sending in their own governors and civil servants, as Britain did in Kenya and India. In South America, the Middle East and Africa it used bribery to destroy governments who resisted its trading terms, usually with British support. It surrounded the old Soviet Union with American air force bases from the Arctic Circle round to Turkey, including nations in the North Atlantic Treaty Organisation – NATO. These are almost wholly manned by American servicemen commanded by the USA, and are a new kind of colonist. Like those manning the American nuclear submarine base off the Firth of Clyde, they were at first meant to defend the rest of the world from attack by the Soviet Union, and are now supposed to defend it from international terrorists. In the 1970s the USA withdrew their air force base from Greenham Common, partly because a lot of brave English folk, the most notable of them women, protested by camping round it. The NATO base on the Isle of Lewis has aroused no local protests the British press and broadcasters think worth reporting. The local economy must be slightly boosted by these colonists.

Scotland has never had more than a tenth of England's population but the proportion of Scots leaving to settle in other lands has been notorious for centuries. In the Middle Ages the French said, 'Rats, mice and Scots can be found everywhere'. Adventurous people in poor countries have often sought a better life in richer ones, even when not driven from their homelands by famine, as in nineteenth-century Ireland, or by greedy land-lords in the Scottish Highlands. Our most famous emigrant was James VI of Scotland who became James I of England, when the Catholic Irish were yet again trying to throw off English government. Mainland Britain was most open to Irish inva-sion across the narrow straight between Galway and Galloway – between Ulster and Scotland. By force of arms Jamie drove Catholic landowners out of Ulster and offered their properties to Protestant settlers from Scotland and England, a settlement that led to future civil warfare. Many more Scots than English took advantage of his offer because more Scots saw that leaving their homeland was a way to enrich themselves. And like King Jamie, Tony Blair and other politicians, Scots have prospered by settling in England. This was made possible for many Scots because till recent times the northern nation had a higher stan-dard of public education for its poorer classes. Doctor Johnson voiced strong anti-Scottish opinions, but most of those he employed to his make his dictionary were Scots.

The rulers of rich countries have often tried to get richer still by invading poorer lands, hence Boss William of Normandy's conquest of England, and the conquest of Ireland by his descen-dants. The many clans and peoples north of Hadrian's Wall only became one nation through resistance to continually renewed efforts by the southern government to subdue them. In 1707, during what is now called *a severe economic depression*, the main owners of Scotland were paid to become a tenth part of England's parliament. For over two and a half centuries colonists and settlers from Scotland – and Ireland – helped the London government to establish and administer a British Empire. Meanwhile throughout the eighteenth and nineteenth century the Scottish lowlanders cultivated their most fertile districts and used local deposits of iron and coal to develop their own industries, and made Scotland a centre of world trade, exporting more manufactures than its people. Those in the Highlands and Western Isles were unluckier for more reasons than can be mentioned here, but landlords who (sometimes helped by the army and police) evicted most of their tenants were mostly guilty, at first because they made more money by using their estates for sheep, then by renting them or selling them to wealthy southerners who enjoyed shooting and fishing there. After north Britain became reachable by railway and steam ship many southerners began coming here, and have been coming ever since.

But after 1918 they came to a Scotland managed by folk who increasingly thought of their homeland as a province, as eighteenth and nineteenth century industrialists, scholars, scientists and authors had not. This was because the Scottish iron and shale oil deposits were exhausted, and a generation of brave and intelligent new minds had been killed or damaged in the First World War. After the Treaty of Versailles came more and more unemployment. This was worsened by Scotland's potentially strongest administrators and publicists going to work in London or overseas, leaving their homeland to those who had no confidence in any local who was Scottish, unconventional, and proposed or wrote things London might not appreciate. This did not discourage immigration into Scotland from what were or had been parts of the British Empire, and Ireland, and most of all England. By the 1970s the long list of Scots doing well in the south was over balanced by English with the highest positions in Scottish electricity, water supply, property development, universities, local civil services and art galleries.

Immigrants into Scotland, as into other lands, are settlers or colonists. English settlers are as much a part of Scotland as Asian restaurateurs and shopkeepers, or the Italians who brought us fish and chips. The colonists look forward to a future back in England through promotion or by retirement. Said Scott Fitzgerald, 'Start with an individual and you may end with a type. Start with a type and you may end with... nothing'. I will speak of individual immigrants known to me. Because I am a writer in Glasgow they are all associated with literature and the arts, but I think Scottish folk in other professions will know settlers and colonists with similar attitudes. I will start with a colonist.

In the mid 1980s I met Michael Goldberg, an English talks producer in BBC Glasgow who was going to broadcast my story *Five Letters From an Eastern Empire*. He told me he had been an advisor on science broadcasting in London BBC until 1977, when a referendum looked like giving Scotland its own parliament. Since this would have enlarged the scope of Scottish broadcasting, he had been sent here with others to take charge of it. But a clause in the referendum bill (inserted at the last minute by a Labour MP) resulted in the majority voting for a Scottish parliament being too few to get it. Unlike the others he remained in Glasgow, and was now in charge of broadcast talks. He asked who I would like to read my story, which is told in the voice of an oriental poet laureate. I said it would be easy for Bill Paterson. Mr Goldberg said, 'But the speaker is supposed to be the poet laureate of a *mighty empire* and Bill Paterson has a Scottish accent!' I agreed with him but explained that my poet was a mandarin, and the Scots also had a mandarin accent used by many of our headmasters and heads of departments, accents quite different from those of Oxbridge. Mr Goldberg did not understand that, so my story was broadcast from London by an English actor using the Queen's English.

Today Scotland has the parliament it did not get in 1977 and certainly the London BBC has taken firmer control of broadcasting here. When members of that parliament suggested Scotland should have its own news broadcasts the BBC chief here said Scotland (whose population equals that of Denmark and Israel, is larger than that of Norway and the Irish Republic) does not generate enough news to justify such broadcasts. The British Broadcasting Corporation certainly wants to make sure that it never will.

Mr Goldberg was a colonist. Had he not died in a train crash when commuting between Edinburgh and Glasgow, he may have become a settler, though one who regarded Scotland from a London perspective. Many Scots have the same view of their country, especially those in the New Labour Party, who invited English administrators north when Margaret Thatcher's government made Glasgow Britain's first European City of Culture.

Glasgow had staged four great international exhibitions between 1880 and 1937 in which the city and Scottish culture were strongly represented, but in those years Scotland had not been thoroughly provincialised. For 1990 the Labour Council that had ruled Glasgow almost continuously for sixty years hired the best English arts administrators money could rent, and gave them control of Glasgow's main concert halls, theatres and galleries. They could have staged a drama festival of successful plays by Glasgow-area authors – Bridie's *Mr Bolfry*, McLellan's *Jamie the Saxt* and Ena Lamont Stewart's *Men Should Weep*. Archie Hind's Scottish version of *The Ragged Trousered Philanthropists* could have been staged with its original producer, David Hayman. They could have got an original stage play by commissioning John Byrne and Peter McDougall, successful stage and television authors, to co-operate with Billy Connolly to create something new, as the *Great Northern Welly Boot Show* was created. They could have arranged shows of paintings from those late nineteenth-century artists called The Glasgow Boys through the school of colourists around J.D. Fergusson, taking in the best work of those twentieth-century individualists John

Quinton Pringle, James Cowie, Robert Colquhoun, Robert MacBryde and Joan Eardley. But these transient administrators knew or cared nothing for these local achievements and were employed by equally ignorant or careless town councillors. To both sorts the city's past was mainly rumours of gang violence and radical Socialism, both of which should be forgotten. New Labour wanted the City of Culture to attract foreign tourists and investors, so performances and shows were brought from outside Scotland. Hardly anything Glaswegian was presented in Glasgow's Year of Culture.

But other arts administrators were invited to Scotland by the Scots, stayed longer but were still colonists, not because they eventually retired to England or were promoted to other jobs there, but because their work for institutions originally created to encourage art in Scotland actually depressed it.

When Yeats and Lady Gregory established Dublin's Abbey Theatre they were not interested in Oscar Wilde and Bernard Shaw's plays which did well in London's West End. They started a tradition of Irish playwriting which still flourishes, so that Ireland (as an American told Roddy Doyle) 'punches well above its weight' as a centre of international literature. Before the Second World War there were many unsuccessful Scottish efforts to follow the Abbey Theatre's example, and immediately after it the playwright James Bridie thought the Glasgow Citizens' Theatre had achieved this. Subsidised by Glasgow City Council it successfully produced Scottish plays by Bridie, MacClellan, Joe Corrie and others between great plays by Shakespeare, Ibsen, O'Casey, Brecht, Frisch and Irishmen from Synge to Friel. That Citizens' also gave a start to fine actors, Duncan Macrae and Helen Mirren among them. In 1969 Giles Havergal became director and for thirty-four years produced excellent plays that drew full houses, only two of them plays by Scots with Scottish settings. This policy of exclusion was supported by Jan McDonald, a member of the Citizens' board and lecturer in drama at Glasgow University, who was outspoken in her belief that Scotland would never produce a good dramatist. Nor did the theatre under Giles promote Scottish acting, since out-of-season he planned and auditioned for his productions in his London home.

When the Scottish Arts Council started after World War Two its chief members were James Bridie the playwright and the novelist Naomi Mitchison who had alternate meetings in hotel rooms in Glasgow and Edinburgh, with a secretary as almost their only bureaucracy. There is no room to describe how the Council became bigger and operated from Edinburgh but in 1974 it funded The Third Eye arts centre in Glasgow with the director Tom McGrath, playwright, musician and one of the team behind the success of *The Great Northern Welly Boot Show*. Under his guidance it became (said the *Guardian*) 'a shrine of the avant-garde'. Exhausted by promoting the work of Scottish artists and writers while introducing others from abroad, Tom retired after five years to concentrate on his own art. The Arts Council then appointed Chris Carrell who, after a brave beginning, made his job easier by putting others with English qualifications in charge of the centre's exhibitions – people without much knowledge of, respect for the art here, so no local artists spoke up for The Third Eye Centre when Chris directed it into bankruptcy in 1992. However, he gave work experience to English arts administrators who went on to jobs in the south.

With Scottish Arts Council help the National Theatre of Scotland was founded in 2005, with its main office in Glasgow. Vicky Featherstone, its first artistic director, may be leaving in 2013 for work nearer London. That is my only reason for thinking her a colonist. But for at least forty years before our National Theatre was created several theatre companies, many theatre productions and many literary magazines depended for their existence upon Scottish Arts Council subsidies, which were withdrawn by a well funded bureaucracy that never thought to economise upon itself. In 2010 it gave way to a Quasi

Independent Non-Government Organisation called Creative Scotland which aims to invest in

> Scotland's arts, screen and creative industries

because

> It's our job to help Scotland's creativity shine
> at home and abroad.

The appointed director was not Scottish, admitted to knowing nothing of Scottish culture, but said he was willing to learn. Ain't Scotland lucky? And if you feel these former remarks are full of anti-English prejudice, remember that these colonists were invited here and employed by Scots without confidence in their own land and people.

Let us think of settlers here who became more effectively Scottish than most born natives. One was Edward Dwelly, a Welshman who learned Gaelic, wrote the first reliable and complete Gaelic dictionary, and raised the money for publication in 1911 after typesetting and printing it by hand himself. Another was Frank Newbery from Devon, the director of Glasgow School of Art who got Mackintosh the commission to design his greatest building, and supported him when he was ostracised by other Glasgow architects. Still here is Timothy Neat, the Cornishman who lectured on design at Dundee College of Art. By writing books, committee work and original film production he has promoted and commemorated the works of Hugh MacDiarmid, Hamish Henderson and Sorley MacLean – strong Socialists often disparaged when not deliberately ignored by Scotland's media and officialdom because the first two were also ardent Nationalists and the last a Gaelic poet. Timothy's film *The Summer Walkers*, inspired by Henderson's collections of contemporary folk song, beautifully records a phase of twentieth-century working life in Scotland before it passed away, as such life always passes, but it is too modern to be mere nostalgia. Timothy has also promoted the work of John Berger, another Socialist and European author, for his interests are worldwide.

David Knowles and Sharon Blackie, he a former air force pilot, she a psychologist, became crofters on the Scottish west coast. In 2006, using laptop technology, they started The Two Ravens Press to publish books they liked; I met them because they successfully published two of mine. In May 2012 they brought out the first number of *EarthLines,* a thoroughly professional good-looking magazine (price £4.99) devoted to articles and fiction about *Nature, place and the environment.* This magazine is for readers throughout Britain, but their croft in Lewis is not a hobby. They keep a flock of sheep, two pigs and a cow. David has dug drains that channel their sanitary waste into the soil. In plastic tunnels Sharon grows their vegetables. David has learned Gaelic and is working with others in nearby crofts to fence off the huge area of common moorland allowed them by the nineteenth-century Crofting Acts. Crofters in the past have lost control of land because they did not co-operate to assert their rights to this common property.

David and Sharon probably came here because a Scottish croft cost much less than an English smallholding. The comparative cheapness of Scottish property has led other southerners to run small businesses here, mostly in catering. Some annoy nearby caterers by service that attracts more customers. This must lead to improvement. Years ago an official enquiry into Scottish catering declared that many owners 'had an almost suicidal disregard for their customers' wishes'. I do not know or care if the true settlers I have mentioned will vote for Scottish independence in the 2014 referendum, as I certainly will. Their work here is good for us.

Only one question should be asked by that referendum: Do we who live in Scotland want an independent government? The present state of Britain is bad for many in the south as well as the north. Although the Tory and Labour parties in London who brought this about still pretend to differ from each other, both unite in wanting to keep control of Scotland. Their Ministries of Information and Misinformation are already working openly or subtly to divert us from that one question. To ask us if an independent Scotland should keep its NATO bases is trivial and irrelevant. In Washington the countries in NATO are jocularly called 'Snow White and the Twenty-Seven Dwarves'. Recently three of the dwarves (the German, Dutch and Belgian governments) suggested that Snow White remove her bases from their soil. With the backing of Britain and other NATO dwarves, Snow White said she would not. Before Scotland has an independent government, whether it sides with Germany, Holland and Belgium in this matter is irrelevant.

KIRSTY GUNN

In Sutherland, over the Jubilee weekend this June, I saw nothing but bunting. Strings of flags in the colours of the union jack were threaded through the little high streets of Brora and Rogart, bunting and flags filled shop windows in Golspie and Dornoch. All red, white and blue, red white and blue… It fluttered gaily and thoughtlessly in our fine, early summer wind.

We had no bunting ourselves – but then we fly no Saltire either – in our highland home in the hills. I was born and brought up in a Britain, in a Scotland, far, far away, one might think, from all this, on the other side of the world, even, and they talk about 'independence' there too, but we had our bunting as well. The Queen came to visit. That was her head on the stamps we used.

Christmas is in summer, in that other Scotland I grew up in, and Burns Night, too, and the 'Highland Games' are held in places with names like *Waipu* and *Rotorua*. Still, I spent my child-hood listening to the sound of the bagpipes as my father and his friends tuned up and played *piobaireachd* on wooden stages especially built for the occasion, while in the next paddock burly men in kilts tossed the caber and wee girls in woolen hose and black laced pumps did their criss-cross dancing over swords that flashed bright in the Antipodean sun. I am there-fore, understandably, confused over issues like 'identity' and 'nationalism' and 'independence'. Independent from whom, or what? After all, what country is ever, truly, on its own?

Yet being alone is something we value, isn't it? Our cultural story tells us that it is the loner who is the individual, unfettered by the claims of others and the need to behave and to conform. The loner is the hero, the leader, the prophet, the poet. The one who claims her heart's desire without playing by the small rules; she's the one who goes her own way. To be alone is to be at peace with one's place in the world, untroubled by worldliness… It's a definition that's held good for centuries, and so when I think of independence in these terms, the country that might describe itself this way does not exist. It would be a place for books, for poems, that Scotland, maybe. And for the politicians' speeches, of course. But it's nowhere we can go and live.

I've been thinking about all these issues a great deal over the past eight years, while I have been at work on a fictionalised account of a Highland family who see themselves very much as independent, cut off from the rest of Scotland, even, with a musical tradition that marks them as separate and set apart, and they are quiet with it, this group of individuals, invisible some might say, and self-regarding and self-sufficient. Yet their own family story is in fact deeply and richly interconnected with a past – a culture, a family heritage – that they could never abandon. For they have a place they call 'Home' – a particular house, a dot of land upon the hill. And with that at your back, is the understanding I have come to in writing this book, with a clear sense of where one has come from, and so then how one can be defined … How could that ever reflect independence, in the end? If the child who might leave might also come home again? If the solitary traveler might have had his destination waiting for him all along?

At the end of the day, my sense of who we are comes, not from the politicians' rhetoric – ideas of nationhood and self-determination and a Scottish Parliament and all the rest – but from what we do, how we were raised. Those 'Highland Games' of my childhood – and there were no quotation marks around the words when we said them then – defined me as a Scot as much as my Scottish School did, with its Houses called Braemar and Berwick and Loch Leven, and my Caithness Granny's tablet and the ceilidhs that were held, in our house or in halls and theatres, or at the Burns Suppers and St Andrew's night dinners I attended.

It was given to me, that identity, in the books I read – Neil Gunn and George Mackay Brown – and in my father's *piobaireachd* that I heard… In the Thurso magazine to which I contributed stories and poems… In my aunt's highland dancing classes, in her strathspeys and reels…

And in the hills we walked on, then, in the Southern Hemisphere, that reminded us, we said, of 'home.'…

Yes, there'll be plenty who say we need this other imagined 'independence'. That we need our own land back and our governance like we needed the oil that came out of our seas and the industry that came out of our factories. They'll say the quiet parts on our map are quiet for reasons that we should not forget, that it's time for people and industry and a vigorous self-governed economy to get busy in the still expanses of our landscape, that there was stillness enough after the clearances, when nothing moved at all across the hills except the sheep. There'll be plenty who say that an empty landscape is a land-scape of poverty, and that the whirr of economy and industry, the endless turns of the white wind turbines that we are seeing more and more of across the far hills, supposedly to bring us energy and sustainability, means money for Scotland and power again, like perhaps we had some power once.

But the power is here all around us, in what we love, in what we make, in our art and literature and in our intellectual and cultural lives. In what we already have.

Right now, they are starting to put up the bunting over the fairgrounds of Helmsdale and Tain for those other Highland Games that don't need speech marks around them. And in the end, it doesn't matter to me what colour it is. It may as well be the New Zealand flag they're flying for as much as I can ever know about the world through politics and pinched ideas of race.

It's how we imagine ourselves and the country around us that makes us who we are, independent in a way that's true and strong and real. Never the other thing. That other gets turned into a different slogan, is bought and sold every day and, unless we willingly choose, it could never lay claim to those lonely, lovely hills that speak to me of somewhere that's both separate and connected, a place where I myself might live, where I might belong.

KATHLEEN JAMIE

I'm not a one for hoarding but I do have one small souvenir from the devolution days of the 1990s. I can't remember how I came by it, probably at a demonstration.

It's just a white polythene bag, with a blue Saltire printed on one side. If you carry it with that side facing out, folk might take you for a tourist who's just bought a tin of shortbread. However, writ large on the other side is this:

```
DESTINY
        -Find your own stone.
```

Worked round the edge are other phrases:

```
folk        place       work
air         stone       equilibrium
body        mind        spirit.
```

And, at the bottom, this:

```
CAUTION: Don't pull this Destiny Bag over
your head. It is for the conveyance of the
natural energies of the Individual, Community
and the Planet. Inorganic political and
economic impurities will damage the bag and
nullify the Synergic Guarantee. Suffocation
is bad for you.
```

It was designed by George Wyllie who died this year and I'm sorry he's gone because we need his like. There's fun in this bag, a wry joke against ourselves and references which everyone understood at the time. (It's dated 1992, four years before the Stone of Destiny was piped and pomped back to Scotland in one of the decade's more bizarre events.)

Time has passed and I'm middle aged now but I'm sure there was a natural energy and a civic and artistic energy 20 years ago which has dissipated; a Scottish collectivism I don't sense much any more. There were some great minds in the Labour party then, but for the most part our politicians were cowerin' in Westminster under Margaret Thatcher and her successors. We had a 'democratic deficit', which was exciting, and political vision had devolved to the people: trades unions, churches, writers. With no spin or party line and no centralised control, the country was wittier, fresher, more angry. More inclined to imagine and to think. We queried ourselves. We generated more synergy.

It seems to me that today's Independence 'debate' is being handed down to us by career politicians so it immediately feels inauthentic. Full of inorganic political and economic impurities, you might say. There is no fun around it, that's for sure. No pawky self-examination, no roaring dissatisfaction. Because we, the people, sense its falsity, we are not thinking and dreaming. Instead of dreaming a nation, we're reduced to fretting about 'the economy'. We're in danger of believing that if we just stick the weary word 'Scottish' in front of the same old thought-patterns, the same institutions, we will have achieved 'independence'.

But it looks like a referendum will happen, so what we need are new Destiny Bags, so we can take the whole thing out of the politicians' grasp and carry it ourselves. Starting now, we need to imagine yet again the kind of Scotland we want. It's no bad thing to keep imagining and testing one's ideas, and we have a younger generation now, mere babes in 1992, who have never known how energising that national dreaming can be.

What kind of Scotland do we want? Och, nothing fancy:

One with a bit of social justice. Which exerts some democratic control over the country's major assets, including land, which in turn would improve the self-esteem and therefore health of its citizens. Which raises taxes to provide education, healthcare and opportunity regardless of social class. Which requires respected and respectful social services. Which seeks to eliminate child poverty, and appalling housing. Which extends a decent hand to immigrants and asylum-seekers. Which guarantees freedom for the arts and culture, and a knowledgeable and enthusiastic mechanism for subsidy (not 'investment', artists can't operate on a business model). Which is served by an intelligent media, respectful of women. Which gives a damn for the natural world and the furtherance of the other species inhabiting Scottish land and waters. Which harbours no weapons of mass destruction.

That kind of thing. Individual, Community and Planet.

Even if the 2014 referendum goes off at half-cock, as it might because our Synergic Guarantee has been nullified, I'll have to vote yes. That's because I can't now see any other way to clear the space we need if we are to become a mature and self-determining country. We've been conned into believing that it's impossible to fashion public policy out of common decency. This is not proven, we can try, and I think now that independence is the most likely route to that end. It's a long road for a short cut, as my father would say.

Like many Scots, I can clearly distinguish between independence and nationalism, and I wouldn't be voting for nationalism, certainly not for tartan-la-la. Really I'd want a yes vote, then a bloodless coup the next morning before there were any flags or triumphalism.

Any triumphalism, and I'll pull my Destiny Bag over my head.

JAMES KELMAN

In an American journal I read a prominent English writer was described as 'very British'. What can it mean to be 'very British'? Could I be described in this way? Can my work be described as 'very British'? No, not by people in Britain, or by those with a thorough knowledge of the situation. The controlling interest in 'Britishness' is 'Englishness'. This 'Englishness' is perceived as Anglo-Saxon. It is more clearly an assertion of the values of upper-class England, and their validity despite all and in defiance of all.

Power is a function of its privileged ruling elite. To be properly 'British' is to submit to English hierarchy and to recognise, affirm and assert the glory of its value system. This is achieved domestically on a daily basis within 'British' education and cultural institutions. Those who oppose this supremacist ideology are criticised for not being properly British, condemned as unpatriotic. Those Scottish, Welsh or Irish people who oppose this supremacist ideology are condemned as anti-English. The 'British way' is sold at home and abroad as a thing of beauty, a self-sufficient entity that comes complete with its own ethical system, sturdy and robust, guaranteed to outlast all others.

British people are led to believe that the Royal Family are admired, loved and glorified across the globe. Should another Solar System contain life upon any of its myriad planets its inhabitants will not only accede to the Christian church but acknowledge the Head of the English Royal Family as Defender of the Faith, in competition with the Pope, standing next in line to God.

Writers like myself are guilty of being 'too Scottish'; our 'Scottishness' is as an attack on 'Britishness' and acts as a disqualification. It is assumed that Scottish experience is homogenous whereas English experience offers a wide-ranging and worldly heterogeneity. Our work is attacked in pseudo-literary tones for its perceived insularity. This also happens within Scotland; anglocentric Scottish critics condemn Scottish writers for their 'lack of diversity'.

Being 'too indigenous' is the same as being 'too working class' and, predictably, the closer we move to the realm of class the clearer we find concerns of race and ethnicity. No one remembers that 'Briton' has something to do with Celticness. Being 'too Scottish' is seen as an assertion of a Celtic rather than Anglo–Saxon heritage. The marketability of certain individuals derives from the arousal of this racial stereotype. The *proof* of the English footballer David Beckham's marketability is in his Anglo-Saxon 'provenance'.

A colonial or imperial context helps clarify the argument. The key is class. 'Scottishness' equates to class and class equals conflict. Even within Scotland we can be criticised for this. The work of writers deemed 'too Scottish' shares a class background. Occasionally we are condemned for *confining* our fiction to the *world of the urban working class*. This suggests that for working class people cultural boundaries are fixed in place. Their world is an entirety of experience, culturally as well as economic. None can step beyond the limits of that world. It is a world barren of the finer things in life which are not only material but spiritual. Working class people cannot engage with art and philosophy. In their world there is no art and philosophy.

This elitism is straightforward and at the heart of the hostility but, as with racism, is seldom remarked upon within the establishment and mainstrean media. It rarely occurs to critics that working class people might read 'proper' books or look at paintings as opposed to 'pictures on the wall'. When it does occur to them it is treated as a phenomenon. They do not progress to the discovery that the life of one human being is as valid as another, that the life experience of one section of society is as diverse as another.

The bourgeoisie tend to go with the colonisers and the imperialists as a means of personal and group survival, and advancement. They quickly buy into the culture of the ruling elite. Indigenous languages and cultures are kept alive by those at the lower end of society. In India and much of Africa, as well as Australasia and North America, the voice of authority continues to be English. The lower order groups keep alive the local, the richness of the indigenous languages, the indigenous aesthetic, the culture – as best they can, not necessarily by choice or intention. The proletariat and other lower order groups do not have much of a choice. Typically education is denied them, their languages and cultural markers are proscribed, regarded as weapons. To use these language or cultural markers is seen as cultural vandalism or acts of terrorism.

Since the eighteenth century the cultural and linguistic movement of the Scottish bourgeoisie and ruling elite is total assimiliation to Britishness where Englishness is the controlling interest. Scotland has its own languages too, and these are 'living languages', kept alive by people using them who, generally, are working class. Scottish literary artists have worked in these languages for centuries. Even where the writers are not themselves working class in origin the subject matter of the work is, as we see in some of the writings of Walter Scott or R.L. Stevenson.

Scotland also has its own philosophical, legal, religious, literary and educational traditions, and most of this too is marginalised. Scottish educators have to fight Scottish institutions to find a place for Scottish philosophy, literature and education itself. Many English people sympathise with the plight of Scottish culture; they see cultures and traditions marginalised everywhere, and recognise also the plight faced by people from Yorkshire, Cornwall, Northumbria, Cumbria, Somerset, Lancashire and so on.

The difference is that Scotland is not an English county, it is a British country. It will continue to be a British country whether or not we are governed from London, England. This is because Great Britain is a geographical entity. It is a mistake to attribute particular sensibilities or character traits to the millions of people who live in its countries of Wales, England and Scotland. And then there is the north of Ireland.

People are right to treat nationalism with caution. None more than Scottish people who favour self-determination. Any form of nationalism is dangerous, and should be treated with caution. I cannot accept nationalism and I am not a Scottish Nationalist. But once that is said, I favour a 'yes or no' decision on independence and I shall vote 'yes' to independence.

Countries should determine their own existence and Scotland is a country. The decision is not managerial. It belongs to the people of Scotland. We are the country. There are no countries on Mars. This is because there are no people on Mars. How we move ahead here in Scotland is a process that can happen only when the present chains are disassembled, and discarded, when the majority people seize the right, and burden, of self-determination.

The Nationalist Party has exposed its weakness in this area. Under their leadership 'independence' may be distinguished from 'self-determination'. In his speech of January 25 2012 Alex Salmond declared: 'With independence we will have a new social union with the other nations of these islands and will continue to share Her Majesty the Queen as Head of State'. This returns us to the seventeenth century when the ruling elite in Scotland retained their own Parliament but shared kingship with England and Wales. During this period all major policy matters concerning army and international affairs were settled not by the so-called 'Scottish Parliament' but in the Palace of Westminster. That so-called 'Scottish Parliament' belonged to such a tiny group of aristocrats, landowners and corrupt placemen that there is little point discussing it when we refer to the issue of self-determination. The majority Scottish people have never experienced self-determination at any time in history.

I am not a patriot. A 'patriot' is one who accepts national identity as grounds for a primary solidarity. It is patently absurd that the majority people should expect solidarity from the ruling elite and upper classes. In Scotland there is no justification for such a hope let alone expectation.

The British establishment left, right and centre are as one in their opposition to Scottish self-determination. This applies to the many Scottish politicians of the Tory Party, the Labour Party and the Liberal-Democrat Party who 'cross the political divide' to stand together in defence of the Union. It is useful to see this priority expressed so clearly. This type of united front is common in situations of war.

For many people, not only career politicians, a benign paternalism is preferable to independence. A similar choice is faced by adolescents. Should we leave home and live as self-determining adults or stay home and enjoy the comforts provided by mum and dad?

The Scottish Nationalists' push to subject the majority people to a Royal Family pays homage to another tradition associated with 'Scottish identity': submission and servitude to the ruling elite. Manna for Empire builders and Colonialists. Dependency is at the root of this aspect of 'Scottish identity'. There may be a 'right' of self-determination; on the other hand there may not. Even if there is such a right it need not be exercised. Siding with the imperialist is a better option: dogs brought to heel can be robbed of their bones.

Scottish people are encouraged by the establishment to take pride in their service to the Monarch, the Royal Family and all of its subjects. Scottish children are taught to glorify submission and servitude, embodied in the myth of 'the Scottish soldier who wandered faraway and soldiered faraway', in the retention of British authority and the denial to the majority people both foreign and domestic, of the right of self-determination.

There are centuries of imperialist myth-making, misinformation and propaganda to disentangle. Clan allegiance has been strong in the highlands and islands of Scotland, as has religious difference throughout the country. This continued throughout the seventeen and on through the eighteenth century until the Battle of Culloden in 1746 when the clan system and Jacobitism were effectively destroyed.

The British State has sought to deny the right to self-determination consistently over the past few hundred years in Africa, the Americas, Ireland, the Indian Sub-continent, South East Asia or Australiasia. The State has used every argument it can to cling onto power and when necessary applied the requisite dirty tricks, and finally moved in the army to achieve their objective, at whatever cost, including the slaughter of innocents.

Unfortunately religious difference remains significant into the twenty-first century. The Scottish Nationalists' support for such an intrinsically British institution will appear as a sop not only to Unionist sympathisers but to 'the Protestant vote'. This opens a nasty sore on the Scottish political and cultural scene. Traditionally, Protestants are anti-Republican Unionists who regard the King or Queen of England as Defender of the Faith. Roman Catholics are believed to favour Republicanism. In Scotland many people confuse 'Republicanism', 'Roman Catholicism' and 'Irishness'. Some believe them to be one and the same thing. The subtext to their pro-Unionist, anti-Republican stance is sectarian racism: anti-Catholic anti-Irish. Others in Scotland will view the Nationalist retention of the British Monarchy in these terms.

To what extent religious sectarianism will play a part in the move towards independence is unknown but few politicians will want to become embroiled in this. The Nationalists have stated elsewhere that they are in favour of lifting the ban on Roman Catholics holding the Monarchy. This may set the minds of some to rest.

The continuing debate in Britain is led by the establishment and mainstream media and focuses on whether or not independence is 'good for Scotland'. This is a red herring. It is an argument from self-interest and therefore secondary. The economic consequences of self-determination are important but are not and cannot be the central issue. Experts and specialists debate on the deployment of capital resources; defence and foreign policy, business & industry; health and welfare issues, religions and secularism. Shall Scotland seek to enter NATO, the UN, the British Commonwealth, the European Union? What will happen to 'our' soldiers and 'our' army-towns, 'our' battleships, warplanes, tanks and submarines? What effects will independence have upon our relationships with the USA, with England, Wales and Ireland, not to mention Spain, Italy, Israel, Turkey and all those other countries keeping the lid on their own governance issues.

How we progress as a people will depend on how we contend with those and other matters. A people cannot be asked to settle in advance of independence how they shall act in hypothetical situations. We are being asked to provide *a priori* evidence of our fitness to determine our own existence before the freedom to do so is allowed.

Imperialists and colonisers lay down the judgment that there is no 'right' of self-determination. But that judgment has no place in the twenty-first century. The right to self-determination inheres in every adult human being and distinguishes us from animals, mammals, birds, fowls or fish. No one grants us this right. It is not allowed to us by a benign authority. People exercise the right. It can only be denied to us, as it is denied to the vast majority of the world's population.

Ultimately there is only one issue: the right to self-determination. Underlying the 'good for Scotland' debate is the denial of that right.

People can be subjected to hideous forms of torture and mutilation, and for some it ends in death. This may be rationalised by the perpetrators who deny their victims humanity. Their death carries less value than if the victims were '100 percent' human. Neo-fascism is illustrated where the burden of proof is placed upon human beings to provide evidence of their humanity. Some fall into the trap of accepting the burden of proof. They seek to provide evidence to establish their own humanity. They can only fail. Humanity cannot be 'granted' or 'allowed' them. They already are human. Their humanity is being denied.

We are talking about freedom. We exercise freedom. If freedom be denied us we seize it as our right. No one gives us our freedom. We take it. If it is denied us we continue to take it. We have no choice. If it is taken from us and we allow it to be taken from us then we are colluding in our own subjection.

The Scottish Nationalists pay allegiance to the concept of 'hereditary subjection' (and spiritual degradation), as embodied in the Queen of the British Kingdoms and I find this repugnant. The question is of historical as well as contemporary relevance. People have fought and died for a political freedom inclusive of Republicanism. They would turn in their grave: such as Thomas Muir, John Baird, James Wilson, Andrew Hardie, James Connolly, Arthur McManus, John Maclean. No one has the right to represent the voice of the Scottish people in a matter of such gravity. It is a massive set-back but not insurmountable. It is my belief that the Nationalists' brand of independence should still be grasped. We can learn from the past. Sooner or later the right to self-determination will be exercised by the majority people in my country. When I vote 'yes' to independence I shall be voting towards that end.

TOM LEONARD

tune: *The Caledonian Auntie*

my innermost ground is a musical base	ma innermost grunn is a musical base
its grounding in silence its measure in space	its groundin in silence its measure in space
the word for the image an infinite trace	the word for the image an infinite trace
its sound of its silence my innermost place	its sound of its silence ma innermost place

The local is the international.

The national is the parochial.

KEN MACLEOD

Of all the uncertainties and insecurities that hang over us as I write, the outcome of the Scottish independence referendum looms small. A lot of sudden history could happen between May 2012 and August 2014. If we're spared, though, I can imagine my mixed reactions the morning after if the answer is No. At one level I'll be relieved. At another I'll be thinking: we bottled out, again.

It's no longer an original observation that to be Scottish is to have a divided mind. But it was to me when, many years ago, I read in Tom Nairn's 'Old Nationalism and New Nationalism' a diagnosis of that fault-line (in *The Red Paper on Scotland*, edited by Gordon Brown). The cure Nairn prescribed was, and still is, to bring at last the cultural consciousness of a distinct Scottish identity into line with political reality, through independence. Like when two wheels, long disjoint, grinding at each other's gears, finally click into place, the conjunction would be a relief to all within earshot. And at some level it would, for a moment. But what if the click were the closing of a lock?

In the thirty-seven years since Nairn vehemently and wittily assailed the deficiencies of Scottish culture, that culture itself has repaired most of them. No one can say today that there are no Scottish novels that reflect, and reflect on, modern Scotland. There sometimes seems to be another unmissable book that does just that every month, if not every week. The paradox is that this and all the other artistic flourishing of these decades has happened within the union – often in tension with it, or in opposition to it, but within it nevertheless. The hope that culture would flourish yet more in an independent Scotland is a speculation, which may turn out to be mistaken.

One reason for wariness in this regard is the very public-sector preponderance that underlies Scotland's supposed socially progressive, caring and communal character. Competition on an impersonal market is hard enough, as I know too well, but competition for places and grants in a reinvigorated national cultural apparatus bodes worse. The awkward, the out-of-step, the 'unsound' artist or writer could expect much the same caring, consensual back of the hand as the unofficial striker or the 'work-shy' claimant.

The likely effect on England is likewise dire. The worries I have about the Scottish nation rediscovering itself are nothing compared to the dread I feel about an English awakening. I like England perfectly well as it is: asleep. The political view that the inhabitants of the mainland of Britain would do well to remain in one state is too often conflated, by its friends as much as by its foes, with British nationalism, with the British imperialist interest ('our place at the top table', etc) and with glory in our island story. It might be better to point to a pragmatic common interest in keeping the latent nationalism of the island's constituent nations down.

When I see the 'Fàilte gu Sràid na Banrighinn' sign at Glasgow Queen Street, I don't feel a warmth in my Gaelic heart. The synthetic Sinn Fein-ery of the gesture annoys me. I read it as an attempt to make Scotland seem more foreign to England than it is, which makes me feel I'm being made a foreigner. In an independent Scotland I would be deprived of my nationality. That nationality has nothing to do with loyalty to the British state. Disloyalty is itself part of the nationality.

I come from a peculiar people, twice over. Iain Banks, I've heard, once described me as 'a presbyterian communist'. I had to laugh. I grew up British in 1950-60s Scotland. My schoolboy patriotism was as naive as it is possible to be, straight out of the *Daily Express* and the *Reader's Digest*, the *Eagle* comic and the Biggles books. But to be raised a free presbyterian was to learn, without being told, that the state could not be the final moral authority. The church lauded too many martyrs, some of them rebels in arms, for that. In the 1970s I embraced internationalism. Most of the risks I took as a socialist, slight though they were, came from quixotic sorties or scruples in its honour. Looking back, however, the foundation of my youthful socialist consciousness was built on fresh-poured British concrete: the Road Bridge, the Hydro dams, the new high school, the new towns, the new estates.

We misunderstood the reticent generation that won the world we grew up in. For most of them, the Second World War was revolution enough, more terrible and more liberating than any we might have imagined, and the Welfare State was socialism enough. They wanted to forget the war and enjoy the peace. They never told us what they had been through to get it, or explained why they were so unwilling to risk it. No wonder they seemed to us conservative.

We had no such inhibitions about the post-war settlement, which at that time was in crisis in any event. One of the ways we risked it was with Scottish nationalism. I remember the rash of thistle badges among my contemporaries. I had a mild case of it myself, which took the form of speculating on the possible advantages of Scottish independence for the socialist cause. After some discussion I shelved that without regret, little suspecting that the same callow reckoning would decades later entice many on the Scottish Left who are old enough to know better. Some have gone further, and become – or discovered themselves to be – nationalists by conviction.

The real heart-felt nationalists of my generation have had the last laugh on the likes of me. They vote for a party because they believe in it. The rest of us have become so resigned to voting tactically – holding our teeth and gritting our noses – that it's easy to envy them. And, perhaps, to send our tactical vote their way. But we need to keep a clear eye.

Independence would mean, in the first instance, a loss. Having hitherto enjoyed certain inalienable rights as British citizens, we would overnight find ourselves citizens of a new state, one without so much as a constitution, let alone a tradition of legal respect for individual rights. Scotland has no Magna Carta, no Bill of Rights, no proud tradition of awkward precedent. It has the Declaration of Arbroath, the Covenants, and the Claim of Right – claims of freedom and sovereignty to be sure, but in the name of the nation, the church and the people, not the person. In its empire the British state – with the enthusiastic participation of its Scottish soldiers and servants, from Ireland to Iraq – has trampled on every one of the rights it proclaims for free-born Englishmen. It still does. But it has, by and large, been held to its promises at home – except when the wars (from Ireland to Iraq, again) come home.

The left-wing hankering, whether tactical or sincere, for a Scottish capitalist state strikes me as a consequence of defeat and a guarantee of future defeats. The success of nationalism is a consequence of the failure of the Left, whether broad or narrow. The rise of the SNP is in direct proportion to the failures of the Labour Party, Old and New. It's tempting to argue that if only Labour had put a more left-wing (or right-wing) policy to the voters, these failings wouldn't have happened, and that – if the right (or left) lessons are learned – everything can be put right (or left). This temptation should be resisted. Some reactions can't be reversed.

That recognition is at the root of another layer of left support for independence, that of the modernisers and reformers who felt genuinely betrayed by Tony Blair. If democratic reform of the state at an all-British level is blocked, perhaps independence is a way to unblock it, to the benefit not only of the Scots but of the English, 'at last compelled to face their real conditions of life, and their real relations with their kind'. Though it seems to have forgotten all it once knew about the realities of class power and state power, this section of the Left has a hope and enthusiasm that is impossible to deny and hard to begrudge. To speak of hope in the British labour movement, let alone the Labour Party, leaves even me with a tongue that dries in the mouth.

The uphill task of changing the British labour movement has to be measured against the mountain that would face the Left in an independent Scotland. A national carnival of delirium and division would be only the start of it. The notion that Scotland is a more left-wing or progressive country than England is a delusion, arising solely from its recent decades of dependence on state funding: first in industrial subsidy, then in covering the cracks with post-industrial plaster and paint after the industrial installations were ripped out. The world of 2014 is likely to be less stable, and more fraught, than the world of 2012. Economic crisis, institutional paralysis, and military adventure are its predictable features. In a new state thrown from birth into this sadly probable maelstrom, any who dared put the working-class interest before 'the national interest' would get short shrift.

Writers should think, and think hard, about the consequences for them of being mobilised by – at a minimum – moral coercion into the service of a newly confident nation. Being British as well as Scottish may put some of us in a divided mind, but it can't prevent us from putting our minds to any use we like. We should take a jealous care not to mistake the nation's independence for our own.

AONGHAS MACNEACAIL

As the debate heats up, various 'obstacles' to a self-governing Scotland are seen to be chimerical. What seems impossible to answer coherently is 'why not?' Those who ridicule the idea of an independent Scotland (easy to find in the features and letters pages of our daily press) struggle to avoid seeming to do their own country, and its people, down.

The political union exists at present: we live with its myriad imperfections, many of which would be equally prevalent in a separated state. But those who seek change are able to offer the prospect, at least, of something better.

We must continue to live with emotive terms rather than rational argument in favour of the 'status quo', whatever that may be: the dangers implicit in 'breaking up' or 'separation', and warnings of dire economic consequences, including the loss of key industries and services. All these ominous prognoses come from the perspective of an island formation that exists in an apparent vacuum: Ireland, usefully, being a member of this insulated cluster, offering an example of what can go wrong.

And, yes, the Irish economy has suffered badly from a delirious tsunami of property speculation, leaving repeated scenes (most obvious in rural areas) of unfinished construction slowly descending into decrepitude. Yet friends who have lived through that turmoil insist the underlying economy is sound.

But, having visited Ireland fairly regularly for over four decades, I also see a people with a growing confidence in its own identity. Being Scot, and particularly Gael, I was always made to feel welcome, but 'Brits' were, in the early days, viewed with some reservations. Over the years, though, this has mellowed. As indicator of national confidence, the symbolism of the Queen's visit to the Republic cannot be underestimated. There is a clear sense of such exchanges demonstrating that Ireland is an equal partner, in the community of nations, and no province or client state.

Without looking beyond Europe, there is no shortage of small nations, enjoying greater or lesser degrees of independence, and weathering economic crises to varying degrees of success, but showing no signs of seeking to retreat into past dependencies.

Check the Nordic countries: Denmark (population 5.2 million), with its self-governing dependency, the Faroe Islands (50,000), Norway (5m), Sweden (9.4m), Iceland (320,000), and their linguistically different neighbour Finland (5.4 m): likewise the Baltic and Balkan states, with their cultural distinctions and overshadowing neighbours. In such a motley context, it's hard to argue against the possibility that Scotland (5.2m) could also find, and assert, a distinctive legislative, economic and cultural voice, and live as a politically equal and harmonious partner with its larger neighbour.

Throughout the twentieth century and before, leading Scottish writers have tended to show left-wing and/or nationalist leanings (there are, of course, exceptions). Sir Walter Scott was not only a major poet and pioneering historical novelist, but a dedicated collector of his ancestral Border country folklore (which he drew on for his own writing). But his politics were resolutely conservative and unionist: he was a founder of the Tory *Quarterly Review*. And he would experience the disastrous delights of a banking crisis, which ruined him. John Galt, friend and biographer of Byron, played his imperial part in the colonising of Canada, but, in one of his last novels, *The Member*, attacked corruption in the British political system.

Allan Ramsay, who grew up in rural Lanarkshire (if the son of a lead mine superintendent), also collected traditional material: his own use of the vernacular contributed to its revival, anticipating the Roberts, Fergusson and Burns. His interest in the stage, combined with concerns for what was around him, shaped a pastoral opera, *The Gentle Shepherd*. As a non-practicing Jacobite, who described himself as 'neither whig, nor tory', he chose to absent himself when the rebel Prince wished to decorate him. Those were all eighteenth century figures, but in the nineteenth, Robert Louis Stevenson, having been a socialist in his youth, called himself a conservative, though with an element of self-mocking. His identification with the Scottish landscape and its people prompt speculation that he might have been drawn to nationalism. There were always ambiguities.

In the twentieth century, an interweaving of nationalism and left-wing politics tended to characterise the literary scene, though exceptions can inevitably be found. Born in 1901, in rural Aberdeenshire, Lewis Grassic Gibbon (pen name of James Leslie Mitchell) engaged in political activity, with a clear commitment to deal creatively, and critically, with the social conditions of his times. His *Scots Quair* trilogy, transcending polemic, and using the speech rhythms of his Doric environment, is a classic of modern Scottish literature. Ten years older, novelist Neil Gunn, from Caithness, probably best known for fictionalising the herring industry in *The Silver Darlings*, balanced socialist beliefs with a commitment to Scottish Nationalism. As did his more contradictory contemporary, Hugh MacDiarmid, whose capacity for aye being 'whaur extremes meet' has led to a recent controversy about his having expressed kind thoughts about fascism (at a time when that dogma still seemed more socialist than savage). More typical of the man is his expulsion from the nationalist party for being communist, and from the communist party for being nationalist.

That MacDiarmid's endeavouring a translation of Duncan Ban MacIntyre's 'Praise of Ben Dorain' won the approval of Sorley MacLean should cause no surprise. MacLean had himself elected to 'put my thoughts in a dying language', thereby providing a dynamic creative base for its revival, so the older poet's gesture offered welcome support. There was also a shared political outlook, in that MacLean saw the Soviet Union as the future, until disillusioned by Stalinism. Anti-imperialist, he was, primarily, a Gael, who 'if he is at all a Gael, must love Ireland as well as Scotland'.

But among those major characters, few deserve the epithet 'larger than life' like Hamish Henderson. His meditations on war, *Elegies for the Dead in Cyrenaica*, are the proof we need that this was a very fine poet. But 'Seumas Mór' was an entire cultural embrace in himself: linguist, folklorist, maker of folksongs, activist, educator and enabler. As a British intelligence officer, he accepted the Italian surrender from Marshal Graziani. A love of all things Italian combined with an international socialist outlook drew him to translate the prison letters of Gramsci. His commitment to Scotland was manifest in the sweep of his activities in collecting and promoting folk culture, and in his engagement in left-wing political campaigns – always with the dual Scottish and internationalist perspective.

More gentle in their inclinations to publicly identify with cause, though quite resolute in their leanings, poets like Iain Crichton Smith, wry survivor from a hard Presbyterian strait-jacket, the laconic Norman MacCaig and, experimental to the end, Edwin Morgan, were all global in perspective, yet deeply concerned with their own immediate cultural (in the broadest sense of that word) environment. Morgan, of course, put his money where his faith was by leaving a substantial portion of his estate to the Scottish National Party.

Among Scottish women poets, Naomi Mitchison, of landed stock, was nevertheless a committed socialist, and feminist, and enthusiastic advocate for the Scottish island communities and the Bakgatia people of Botswana. Liz Lochhead has declared her intention to vote 'Yes' for Scottish independence. As founder of the Scottish Poetry Library, Tessa Ransford could be said to have made her statement, but she's also written poems on environmental themes. Meg Bateman, a Scottish Borderer of English parentage, demonstrated her commitment by becoming a fine poet in the Gaelic language. Of the two Lewis women, Mary Montgomery is the more explicitly nationalist: while nationhood is a significant thread in Anne Frater's poetry, she is also drawn to reflect on international issues.

While those named may be only a small sample of recent, or contemporary, Scottish writing, and without suggesting any sense of homogeneity, clear exceptions to the tendency to think leftward and/or autochthonically are relatively scarce. The question that then begs to be asked is whether any underlying factors can be identified.

I have, on occasion, suggested there is value in examining the origins and prevailing influence of the Scottish clan system – essentially as found in the Gaelic Highlands, but with its counterparts in the Border lands (an Act of the Scottish Parliament of 1597 talks of the 'Chiftanis and chieffis of all clannish … duelland in the hielands or bordouris') – and, less evidently, in Ireland. Feudalism may have ossified a reactionary hierarchical structure, but scratch the surface and, even in more recent times, a sense of mutuality was significant. I recall living in a small crofting community (where the land was actually State-owned, and therefore free from the presence, or influence, of 'chiefs') where there was an identifiable, if informal, pattern of mutual obligation.

A Marxist friend's reaction to such apparently wooly-minded romanticism was dismissive – but the word 'clan' simply means 'family' in Gaelic. And while those extended family structures had their hierarchical hereditary arrangements, there were flexibilities, and clearly defined mutual obligations. The consent of followers mattered, but the authority of the clan itself took precedence. *Dùthchas*, its collective heritage, allowed chiefs and their kin the right to settle the land on condition they provided protection and authority as trustees for the people. It seems reasonable to argue that a tendency, in Scotland, to lean towards issues and policies of a leftish colour, is the residue of such historical awareness, leading to an outlook definable as the 'collective imperative'. And we may hope, in a fully self-governing Scotland, that such tendencies (sans hierarchical aspects) be acknowledged, explored and developed for the modern age.

The Statutes of Iona (1609) required, among other provisions, that Highland clan chiefs send their heirs to be educated in Lowland Protestant schools where they 'may be found able sufficiently to speik, reid and wryte Englische'. The intention was to alienate clan leaderships from not only their ancestral language but all associated cultural values. That such policies were effective can be deduced from the poetry of Mairi Nighean Alasdair Ruaidh (Mary MacLeod), unofficial Bard to the Clan MacLeod. Her poem 'An talla bu ghnàth le MacLeòid' (The hall where MacLeod was wont to be) powerfully criticises her chief (to his annoyance) for clear divergence from, and betrayal of, Clan customs and traditions.

Then, following the collapse of the romantically nationalist Jacobite movement, after 1746, clan chiefs and gentry gradually became landlords pure and simple, losing their awareness of, or concern for, the traditional obligations they were expected to contribute to their clans. With a few distinguished exceptions, clan leaderships would demonstrate exactly how little they valued old loyalties during the period of the Highland Clearances.

Even after several centuries of political union with the other British jurisdictions, and decades of adjusting to the requirements of the European Union, Scotland, drawing on Pictish, Brythonic, Norse, Roman and Gaelic traditions as well as Anglo-Saxon, has retained a distinctive legal system, incorporating a considerable degree of Roman Law: jury numbers differ - 15 in Scotland, 12 in England; the age of legal maturity, 18 in England, is 16 North of the Border. There are divergences in property law: the Scottish 'offers over' principle being one of the scarier variants.

Scottish education followed its own particular roads too, though any traces of early Gaelic Bardic schools were eliminated with the puritanical onset of a Presbyterianism committed to educate every citizen to read the Bible alone. But a system couldn't be altogether bad that produced intellectuals of the stature of David Hume and Adam Smith. And Gaels, having survived an education policy designed to consign them to oblivion (the 1872 Education Act failed to acknowledge the language existed), can now draw hope, pride, and satisfaction, from the fact that Gaelic medium education continues to expand, shakily in some quarters, but hugely successful elsewhere.

We are who we are. Scotland has demonstrated a gift for assimilating citizens from elsewhere. If my first language came from Ireland, my surname was brought across the Northern sea from Scandinavia, though its origins may be Greek. Scotland's oldest poem is Welsh: the people of the Gododdin inhabited the Lothian area. No one is certain who the Picts were, but they predated the others, and they must, inevitably, have contributed to who we are. And it shouldn't surprise us that more recent migrants make active contributions, as Scots, frequently as left-wing Scots, to the political life of this nation. We are who we are, and are happy to say: welcome aboard.

KEVIN MACNEIL

Scottish Independence: Four Responses

I. The Storyteller

The storyteller sat before a room full of college students who were shortly to vote for the first time in an independent Scotland. When they asked him for advice on how they might approach this milestone, the storyteller responded:

> Some years ago, an eminent Zen priest was invited to hear a talk being given in a local hall by a famous rabbi who was touring the area. To the surprise of his monks and nuns, he heartily accepted the invitation.
> After the talk one of the monks, curious, asked the Zen priest: "Master, how was it? How could a rabbi have anything to teach one such as yourself? What did he talk about?"
> The Zen priest turned to the monk with a bemused look. "Talk about? I didn't go to hear him talk. I went to see how he tied his shoelaces."

II. Allen Ginsberg
(following *Howl Part III*)

I, Allen Ginsberg, am with you in Scotland
        where the madness is banal and institutionalised
I'm with you in Scotland
        where permission is withheld due to indifference

I'm with you in Scotland
    where ah kent yir glaikit flibbertigibbet mither
I'm with you in Scotland
    where we are blessed with the sure mercy
    of scheming poverty
I'm with you in Scotland agus
    thàinig e a-steach orm an-dràsda fhèin:
        is mise Alba
        (tha mi bruidhinn rium-fhìn a-rithist)
I'm with you in Scotland
        Stevenson, Morgan, MacGillEathain
        Ros is Màiri Mhòr
    hammering it out
    on the same futuristic
    typewriter
    great bards we
    are best admired
    when distant and dead
I'm with you in Scotland
    where your condition is reported on national radio
    between green southern weathers and the thunk white
        polite
    thunk aggression of ethnic cricket
I'm with you in Scotland
    where the cultural cringe bows to reveal—
    the cultural cringe
I'm with you in Scotland
    where you suck for your jollies
    at a ditch-scented poisonous
    depressant with grim determination
I'm with you in Scotland
    serendipitous and lazy and grasping
    well-versed
    in the poetry of onomastics
    of handouts

I'm with you in Scotland
    where you weep in a stained football strip
    o proud underdog with your wild defeated whimper
I'm with you in Scotland
    where you expire in the sonorous
    asthmatic caterwauling of redfaced re-fried
    bagpipe tunes made famous by Burns
    or an advert on tv
I'm with you in Scotland
    where I ache to meditate
    on words like 'Knox' and 'liberty'
    and 'Scottish' and 'Enlightenment'
I'm with you in Scotland
    where I'm scunnered with
    the novelty of the abyss
    the global terror franchise
    where all is spin and oil
    and eloquent cowardice will
    not after all suffice
I'm with you in Scotland
    where you will cleave the Long Island
    cleave brave bonnie peedie wee Scotland
    cleave
    cleave us entire
I'm with you in Scotland
    where the chant still swells
    of vocables Gàidhlig and Scots
    and other and heartfelt
I'm with you in Scotland
    where we hug and tongue and caress England
    under the bedsheets the England that
    snores all night and won't let us sleep
I'm with you in Scotland
    and I am like a graveyard
    very nearly as vast as death and

like death Scotland I lack a clear identity
still I will not worry just give me
a fresh eternity the last one being
too Scottish always promising never
fulfilling
I'm with you Scotland
because listen Scotland
in my mind's eye you emerge dripping from a sea-
    journey
through the clear glens and puddled street-neons
and carcinogenic boulevards
across Europe across America across this world of dust
in tears
you emerge at the door of my new cottage here
way out clear on the far shore
where spent eternity has quietened at last
and I have built an expedient raft
under the false gems of Western stars

III. The Artist

1

Hush. Time's river stills.
Scotland turns ice bright in moon
-light. A cuckoo howls.

Some lives are a white
room, a window, a distant
grey glow of sunrise.

'Any change?' Summer
rain. Sudden cheerful trill, the
beggar's mobile phone.

2

I can see my own (many) imperfections in today's dawn rising over Scotland, the dawn blushing as though acknowledging that she, too, has not attained her potential, as if her first appearance might never be equalled. But I can also see how she is miraculous, empty, enlightened. She rises each day and does her best.

IV. The Edicts of Jock Tamson

Introduction
Not parity of contempt, but parity of compassion.

1

Let us foster compassion for all sentient beings.
– Even the English?
Even the English.
– Even the animals?
Even the animals.
– Even me?
Even you.
– Even that spider?
Even that spider.
– Even that murderer?
Even that murderer.
– I will foster compassion for all sentient beings.

2

Preserve the National Health Service.
– Why?
Because in doing so you preserve life.
– I will preserve the National Health Service.

3

Respect your parents, friends, relatives and all those whose actions are beneficial and selfless and bring about a greater good.
– But what about my enemies?
Respect those whose insight is so profound they see an enemy as a friend, that one day you, too, may see an enemy as a friend.
– I will respect my parents, friends, relatives and all those whose actions are beneficial and selfless and bring about a greater good.

4

Strive to partake of peaceful life, not violent death. Be at peace. Be peace.
– How?
Practise restraint, shun egotism. Learn empathy, deflect ill-will. Confront nothing but confrontation, that you may learn its prejudicial nature. Be skilful in the ways of negotiation. Promote harmony. Be earnest, masterful and energetic in what you do. To gain insight into peaceful ways takes effort and determination but to indulge in hatred, rapacity and aversion is to steal, lastingly, from yourself and others.
– I will strive to partake of peaceful life, not violent death. I will be at peace. I will be peace.

5

Understand. Your welfare is that of the sickest and poorest person in Scotland. Your happiness is that of the most wretched, miserable and seemingly hopeless creature in the land. Act accordingly.
– I understand. My welfare is that of the sickest and poorest person in Scotland. My happiness is that of the most wretched, miserable and seemingly hopeless creature in the land. I will act accordingly.

6

To practise compassion, moderation, tolerance and respect takes exertion. Exert yourself. Study, and practise, benevolence, non-violence and patience. Have integrity and be of sound moral character. Be prepared to make personal sacrifices. Renounce the idea of victory and defeat.

– To practise compassion, moderation, tolerance and respect takes exertion. I will exert myself.

7

Freedom and independence come about through state endeavour and individual effort. Guard and be grateful for your freedom and independence.

– What can I do?

Practise self-control, be pure of heart, considerate and generous. Avoid parochialism, cynicism and meanness. Remember excessive humility and egotism are the same thing. Be proactive, not merely reactive. Turn knowledge to wisdom, turn wisdom to wise action.

– I will guard and be grateful for my freedom and independence.

8

Look after the aged. Learn from them.

They have much to teach about life and death. You, too, may one day reach old age. And you will certainly die. As for time, having seen more of it, the aged have a better understanding of time than you do.

– I will look after the aged. I will learn from them.

9

Question everything.

– Why?

Good.

– I will question everything.

10

Learn what is what. Are merit and material gain the same thing? The superficial and the substantial? Is doing a good deed unseen the same as doing it for public approval? Can you transform the country or the world into a better place if you do not first transform yourself?

– I will learn what is what.

11

To be human is a great marvel. Behave accordingly.

– To be human is a great marvel. I will behave accordingly.

12

Do not glorify Scotland at the expense of other countries. Do not glorify yourself at the expense of others.

Nationalism is a poison that heals when taken mindfully and in appropriate measure but destroys utterly when taken to excess.

– I will not glorify Scotland at the expense of other countries. I will not glorify myself at the expense of others.

13

Learn the meaning and practice of compassion and forgiveness and gratitude, for these are virtues only the truly powerful can command.

– I will learn the meaning and practice of compassion and forgiveness and gratitude, for these are virtues only the truly powerful can command.

14

Learn the actual inherent nature of change.

Everything is perpetual change. Every moment you live is changing you in innumerable tiny ways; your being, your physical features, are in constant flux, like the weather which comes into your daily life as an ever-changing and irremovable

influence. If you want to be the change, you must learn the actual inherent nature of change.
– I will learn the actual inherent nature of change.

You may now take your seat in the Scottish Parliament.

DENISE MINA

We don't really know what independence would bring, how much it will cost or what benefits or problems it will cause. We really don't.

Some of us foresee nothing but sunshine, some of us a blasted heath, but we don't actually know. And yet, ask anyone what they think about independence and they will almost always tell you how they are going to vote; yes or no. A simple binary. State your case and defend it to the death. Definitive statements about what independence would be like are either expressions of hope, or else rational, deductive projections based on evidence. Evidence, to be in anyway useful, must be capable of scrutiny. We have lost the language of questioning.

Here is a fun wind-up tool for anyone with a strong position for or against: ask them for further information. Sample questions:

1. Will we have an Ambassador in Bermuda?
2. Is the concept of a nation-state useful in a globalised economy?
3. Will Spain block our entry to the EU, given the situation in Catalonia?
4. Is the democratic deficit more pronounced in Westminster or the EU?

From my own survey of respondents I have never heard anyone say – *gosh I've never thought about that, I suppose I should find out*. Much less – *I don't know, do you know?*

Respondents will usually try to answer. They will be angry at being questioned, as the religious are. They will feel undermined, as the religious do when questioned. Then they will make assumptions about your position and decide that you are 'against' whatever they are for.

We are trapped in a bind: adversarial, binary discussions are all there is left out there. Political discussions are fights-to-win, not forums for working out. So, the vote, whatever the question on the ballot, will essentially be chucking a brick over a wall and listening to see if it makes a happy noise (grassy thud) or a sad noise (bleedy yelp).

That is what this essay is about: how political discussions have all become adversarial engagements. All discussion is adversarial, adamance now passes for integrity and timorous people avoid political discussions because they're afraid of a Paxman-esque mauling. Saying 'let's have a discussion about Independence' will be heard as 'I think I can win this fight'.

The *Today* programme's coverage of the arts is a perfect example of this. The arts are about exploration and raising questions. Last year Graham Linehan was on to talk about his stage adaptation of *The Ladykillers*. He was surprised by the critic Michael Billington whose contention seemed to be 'this house believes your play is crap'. Linehan actually had the wherewithal to step out of the discussion and ask the host if the arts were suited to the adversarial, binary format used for politics. It was a shining moment. The *Today* production team reacted by cutting the piece short.

Question Time audiences may not feel that they have terribly much in common with Jeremy Kyle's viewers but they are watching essentially the same format: opposing sides are set a series of challenges and questions and the audience will show approval or disapproval for their position. The sole distinction is that the issues on *QT* are abstract and on Jeremy Kyle they are personal. The reason this format works so well is that it engages the audience by inviting them to take a side.

Imagine, if you can, an episode of *Question Time* where a Conservative defers to a Labour MP on an issue because they 'know more about this'. Or Dimbleby only asks the panel member who 'has experience in this area' or has 'really thought about this'. That episode would be regarded as pointless or biased. It would undermine the essential form of the show because *Question Time* is an adversarial engagement. It is not an inquisitorial engagement.

Inquisitorial discussion is an altogether different form and one that has almost been completely lost from our public life. It pre-supposes an open mind, the search for information, a desire to *listen*. It is now a sign of weakness to admit that you are undecided or to wonder about things.

Inquisitorial investigation raises questions it can't always answer. It seeks out people with specialist knowledge in each area. It garners factual information and shows its working out on the page so that it can be subjected to close scrutiny.

Of course, it has its own limitations. It takes time and is subject to unsubstantiated leaps in logic and biased points of origin. Worse, its conclusions are often conditional and complex. It rarely entertains. Inquisitorial inquiry doesn't have celebrities on its panel and it does not lend itself to T-shirt slogans.

But here are three other reasons, more pragmatic, that explain why adversarial inquiry has come to be the dominant form of discourse in public life: most people in public life come from legal backgrounds, it is entertaining and it suits short, modern formats, like Twitter and columnising.

Our legal system is adversarial. Our political system is adversarial. As career changes go, law-into-politics is pretty seamless. In hindsight, Tony Blair's call for an end to yah-boo politics seems to have been more about the size of his majority than any real attempt to change the culture.

Provocative statements and arguments are entertaining. They make great sound bites. They are easy to understand. News reports on PM's Questions will never cover technical answers when there are insults and what passes for banter in the Commons. They have a ready narrative in the characters' back stories – angry Gordon vs. smooth Cameron. Personal insults are emotive, instantly engaging and set up stories yet to come.

Ironically, slagging each other off is a degraded form of adversarial inquiry. True adversarial inquiry actually requires the parties to make arguments, find common ground, concede points and slowly, through back and forth to arrive at the nub of the dispute, which they then present before the audience, or the judge, and let them decide the issue.

Watching a shaky YouTube broadcast of the Christopher Hitchens v. George Galloway debate over the Iraq war was one of the funniest and saddest things I've ever seen on the internet, which is saying something (September 14 2005). It was like watching the death of debating. Both parties began their initial address with historical facts and good points but before either had reached the end of their first fifteen-minute address they had fallen into squally insults and point scoring.

That was what was terrifying about the Iraq war. There was for and against, heroes and surrender monkeys, there was Rumsfeldian obfuscation, deliberate misunderstanding of arguments, wilful blanking of protests by millions of the people paying for it, but there was no discussion.

If we're not careful this will be mirrored in the most profound constitutional change for three hundred years.

Using an inquisitorial approach, the independence debate would include people with economic experience of small countries, constitutional theorists and philosophers. Philosophically, there are massively complex questions to be addressed: how to weigh autonomy against economic stability? Can 'identity' be a value, and if so, can it meaningfully be measured against 'fidelity' as a value?

We could be at the helm of a public, philosophical exploration of, for example, the scope of our social and moral obligations, of the limits of international interdependence, of twenty-first century conceptions of statehood. It could be the start of a new enlightenment.

This is getting a bit dry so I'll tell you a story: this may or may not be true but it's still a great story. (*The names have been made up to protect the stupid.*)

Years ago in the Glasgow High Court, a man had been charged with a sickening assault. Let's say he went to someone's wedding and stabbed the groom's father in the eye with a pencil. That's not true but it makes it a better story. Actually, let's say he went *uninvited* to someone's wedding and stabbed the groom's father in the eye with a pencil. Rude *and* violent.

So, this rude and violent man, who we might call 'Mr Rudeman' (not his real name), was charged and his case was coming up and he summoned his solicitor and sacked him. Mr Rudeman said he was going to conduct his own defence. He had uncovered explosive new evidence in his case and wanted to present it himself in court.

'Oh,' said the solicitor, 'Is that altogether wise? Perhaps a more prudent course of action would be for you to give me this new evidence and I could present it on your behalf?'

But Mr Rudeman was insistent: he trusted no one and didn't want it to leak before he presented it in court. By this point the solicitor, sensing an early lunch, bid his former client good luck and pissed off.

Come the day, and Mr Rudeman took the stand. The Fiscal addressed him: 'Mr Rudeman,' said he, 'I put it to you that on the Saturday night in question you went, uninvited, to the wedding reception and stabbed the groom's father, in the eye, with this pencil, to his injury.'

'And I put it to *you*,' Rudeman pointed dramatically at the Fiscal, 'That you're a well known homosexual *in the Edinburgh area*.'

Mr Rudeman died of old age in jail.

Not really, because that would be quite sad, but for the purposes of narrative completeness and consistency, he popped his clogs in pokey.

He didn't get off on the assault because his defence, while commendably spirited, didn't answer what he was charged with: the twin crimes of arriving at a party with a free bar uninvited (bastard) and stabbing someone in the eye with a pencil (not on).

That story was actually set in the late fifties, when Peter Manuel, the Glaswegian serial killer, did a fair to middling job of conducting his own defence and started a short lived fashion of fools-for-clients. Crazes came and went quite quickly in those days.

My point here is that Mr Rudeman is a man for our age. He understood that shining the light on the other side's foibles is a great tactic, that an insulting headline can defer any and all discussion. He also had adamance on his side, which nowadays, in almost any forum but a legal forum, is a substitute for a case.

That story was set in the fifties, when homosexuality was still illegal, and it wasn't widely reported. It became an apocryphal tale lawyers tell each other when they are heart-sore, to show how stupid their clients can be.

But imagine if Mr Rudeman did that now, if homosexuality was still illegal and he exposed the Fiscal in court. Would the Twitter storm centre on 'UNPLEASANT MAN MISUNDERSTANDS THE ESSENTIAL NATURE OF ADVERSARIAL INQUIRY', or 'FISCAL IS A HOMO'?

Twitter is the perfect vehicle for a rumble. The adversarial form is uniquely suited to shortened discussions, and again this suits our age. Who bothers to read forty thousand words in print when someone will give us the gist of it, adamantly, on Twitter?

This is what is lost: context, consequences, information. Academics are famously rubbish on TV and radio because they

will insist on getting facts right and adding codicils to bald statements. Far better to get a celebrity to make a provocative statement than someone who knows the subject.

The fundamental misunderstanding of the nature, purpose and limitations of adversarial enquiry limits public political discussion to such an extent that it is almost impossible to unpack the question of independence and look at it objectively, rationally, with a cold clear eye. This is so much the case now, that the terms 'discussion' and 'debate' are often used interchangeably.

Instead, most independence debates start with the participants telling the audience what their conclusions are and then trying to get them over to their side. This is not a discussion. This is a membership drive. And the true religious are personally offended if their position is questioned or undermined. The true religious know they are right *despite* evidence, not because of evidence. They cannot be dissuaded by evidence. Facts are the enemy of the true religious because their belief system is based on faith and faith alone. And that's scary because, as has been observed in all cultures, through all time, religious people are prone to rather poor decision-making.

Here's hoping for a grassy thud.

DON PATERSON

A Post-Creative Scotland

I have yet to meet one single serious artist who does not privately hold the word 'creative' in anything but contempt. While artists self-evidently *are* 'creative', they don't regard themselves as such, because they know self-consciousness is the death of art; this is why 'Creative Scotland' sounds like a country thoroughly uncertain if it *is*. As for our '*Year* of Creative Scotland' ... words fail us. Its vapidity and cynicism are one thing – if you click on 'Highlight Events' on the Visit Scotland website, you will see a long list of things that were clearly going to happen anyway – but this idiocy also manages to offend every single other year since the Declaration of Arbroath. As for next year, we can assume the nation plans to slide back into slothful unproductivity. It's also embarrassingly provincial: how would you feel, on touching down in Skopje, of being informed that it was 'The Year of Creative Macedonia'?

Though the misuse of the c-word is, of course, more widespread. One of the reasons I dislike the phrase 'Creative Writing' is that it insults my academic colleagues, who are creative writers too. (In my experience the only kind of tenured writer who likes to use 'creative' of themselves are those who declare that they are happy to draw a wage, but constitutionally unfit to do their share of the admin. Or as Chesterton put it: 'the artistic temperament is an affliction of the amateur.') *Everyone* who makes things with skill, love and imagination is creative.

But for all their loathing of it, there's no doubt that the arts have given the word its appeal. So why shouldn't we sprinkle the creative fairydust around? But does anyone *really* want a piece of 'the creative' as artists experience it? I really don't know if they would like the dreams, or the side-effects of the medication. Most folk can leave their work at their work. What artists often stake on their serious games are their own lives, and rarely is this an intellectual or even a conscious choice. (Poetry, for example, is not a 'calling' but a diagnosis.) This conflation of life and work comes at a price: it's a well-known and grim statistical truth that artists have the highest rate of mental illness among the professional classes. The material explanation is relatively simple. 'Creatives', we now think, have a lower density of dopamine-receptors in the thalamus; this reduces its effectiveness as a contextual signal filter, meaning that a lot more information reaches the cortex than in a normal individual, resulting in highly creative and divergent thought-patterns, and a kind of informational disinhibition of exactly the sort we see in schizophrenia. This would go some way to explain the very high incidence of bipolar manic depression in the order of versifiers, writers and artists in general. Let's all be *creative*? I really don't think so. The sense in which 'creativity' applies directly to the artist is often a vicious one – all-consuming, deleterious to physical and mental health, and frequently fatal.

Trust

Nonetheless, there *could* be a positive side to the broader application of the word. The 'creative umbrella' could, in theory, provide cover for and a means of staging encounters between the two neutrally creative constituencies of arts and business. But this cannot come about without constructing the social arena in which they can take place. True collaboration happens socially, and *between equals*. The Enlightenment was itself fuelled by just such an equalising circumstance: yes, Knox had turned education into a recreational exercise in the absence of anything else to do in the evening; but without the social concentration imposed by the architecture of the Edinburgh tenement forcing people into both socioeconomic and intellectual promiscuity, the kind of fertile interchange that allowed, for several years, the Scottish nation to dream bigger and think more deeply than any other on earth – and end the eighteenth century as the most literate nation in Europe – might well not have happened.

One thing everyone quickly learns from this kind of social interaction is their own limitations – where one *should* and *must* concede expertise, because someone else plainly knows far more than you. After that, after you learn a little humility, you start to learn what the other knows; you share it, you import it into your own discipline. Without that sharpened perspective of social encounter, folk can delude themselves that they are far more expert than they really are, or indulge the illusion of moral or intellectual superiority when all they have is economic leverage.

We should know what we're good and bad at. Creative Scotland is an exquisite exercise in the misappropriation and denial of expertise. The administrative wing of the arts has long failed to accept that artists are not good at strategising, form-filling, and writing business plans: indeed they are the constituency *least* capable of doing so. (One of our finest living novelists recently had a Creative Scotland 'trained official' explain to her that the incomprehensible form 'was no more complicated or humiliating [sic] than applying for benefits' and that going to a bit of trouble was worth it to get 'money for nothing'. Spot the ten things wrong with this sentence.) For years arts funding has been disbursed in a way that hasn't just rewarded the quality of the work, but the kind of administrative skill valorised by the people doing the disbursing. We find this increasingly in the universities: the insistence, from the strong economic power-base of HR and middle management, that form-filling and paper-pushing are *intrinsically* valuable and character-building exercises. The diagnosis is the same: an insidious and growing absence of trust. Wherever one can insert mutual suspicion, one requires the mediation of an official form, and the swift result is late-Soviet bureaucracy. It is therefore in the interests of professional bureaucrats to sow mutual distrust. But what scholars are good at is research. What artists are good at is art. An administrator's job is to let them get on with it. It is currently the very last thing they are inclined to do.

The business advisers and 'arts brokers' of Creative Scotland should never, under any circumstances, be in the position of driving what kind of art or literature is produced by offering extravagant incentives for projects that *they themselves would like to see,* and that would not have spontaneously occurred to the artists themselves. This is medieval patronage, not support. What they want to see, they think, is 'innovation' in art. What they often reward is meretricious novelty in format, often in the form of ill-thought-out interdisciplinary collaboration – rather than in those forms which have proven their equality to human creativity over five millennia of R&D, of streamlining their design in the cultural wind-tunnel. That's to say an apparently modest proposal to write a book or paint a couple of pictures might be a thousand times more 'ambitious' than that idea to shave a haiku into a dog's arse, film the results and project it onto Calton Hill. Real 'ambition' is usually a matter of vision and content, not external form, which is purely a means to an end.

The present situation reminds me of a Serbian aphorism: 'the government are using the carrot-and-stick approach: first they beat us with sticks; now they beat us with carrots'. Carrots, in the form of large cash grants for which artists are invited to compete, do not encourage them to think big, or dream large. What they do is encourage cynicism and second-guessing – because artists are generally very poor. But artists *already* dream large. Our artists *are* the repositories of the nation's creative imagination, and are perfectly capable of imaginative innovation in their own terms. They should be trusted to pursue it. Artists must stop having ideas about what kind of business plans their funders might want to hear; business leaders must stop having ideas about what kind of art artists should be making. (And it really would be better if they desisted from calling themselves 'arts brokers'. This basic error leads them to think they can replace the folk doing the *real* brokerage – the expert publishers, curators, artistic directors and promoters they are currently starving out of existence.)

Art is not a democracy

A couple of years ago I was part of a group set up by one of our most literate MSPs to review literature funding in Scotland. I was honoured to find myself in a room with a handful of the more serious players in the Scottish literature sector. We were, however, assembled to do the empty busywork of visible consultation, and we should have known at the time. The process itself was unprofessional, mendacious, corrupt, and ruined by just the sort of nepotism, autocratic whim and lack of oversight that our final report complained of. Predictably, not one recommendation was directly acted upon, nor received anything but the most anodyne lip-service. The report was charged with providing a strategy. That the one we proposed was summarily rejected was bad enough; perhaps it was the wrong one. But that precisely *none has been seen or enunciated since* is wholly unforgivable.

Tellingly, one of our central proposals – the formation of a kind of Scottish Academy of Letters – was the most violently rejected. Such a National Academy would not only have consolidated an invaluable body of expertise; it would have brought our major Scottish writers living and/or published outside of Scotland (i.e. 90% of them) back into the fold, and acknowledged those who have contributed substantially to Scottish literary culture. (The most prestigious awards our writers receive are almost all given in England. Symbolic acknowledgement may seem a meretricious thing, but in a game so financially and emotionally precarious, where the link between work and reward is so often delayed, broken or incommensurate, these peer-awarded tokens mean a great deal to the man or woman who must somehow find the self-confidence to make the mark on the page, the canvas or the stave.) It could also have arranged financial support for its very poorest members, and crucially, it could provide a ready-made panel of experts to help manage the disbursal of public funds to writers and publishers. Despite our showing that it could cost virtually nothing to run, it was firmly kicked into touch as too expensive – and too 'elitist'. In no other walk of life would such a ridiculous objection arise. But then this is Scotland, 2012: through our determination to marginalise our own experts we have debased and perverted the idea of the democratic intellect.

And as for the need for that consolidated expertise – a small anecdote. There was a young author, English but resident in Scotland, who made an application to a core-funded Scottish arts body for a small grant for new writers. It was still a make-or-break amount of money for her, and would've meant the difference between her remaining in Scotland or moving back in with her parents in Suffolk. The gatekeepers in this case were unqualified to judge. The poet received a letter saying that it had been a very competitive year, and there had been stronger entries. I saw some of those entries and they were, scrupulously, not. More personally galling was the fact that I'd gone to the trouble of writing a careful reference extolling the virtues of this individual. I know very little, but have enough evidence to suggest I may be a reasonable judge of poetry. I decided to publish the author myself, in England, on the list I edit at Picador. Rachael Boast has gone on to be shortlisted for every-thing, and won the two main UK prizes for first collections; she has been hailed by everyone from Carol Ann Duffy to Seamus Heaney as an important new voice. She's now based in Bristol.

But I won't write another reference to that body again; my carefully phrased opinion was entirely disregarded in the sole area where I have any proven expertise. I am certainly *not* arrogant enough to insist that it should have counted! But it should have been disregarded by a peer, not a minor apparatchik brought up to think that all opinions in the arts are of equal value. And while it may have been a tiny amount of money, this one bad decision meant we lost a great potential Scot. Academies enshrine a basic principle, without which all other realms of human knowledge would fail: peer review.

An end to 'creativity'

Just as 'a healthy nation is as unconscious of its nationality as a healthy man of his bones' (Shaw), a confident nation has no need to think of itself as 'creative'. But semi-autonomous nations cannot fully know themselves, as they can't fully partake in that international community which would permit them an honest reflection of their own character and worth. We currently seem to know that we are somewhere in size between the Isle of Man and Germany, but tend to act like one or the other, rather than anything sensibly in between.

So what's to be done? Firstly, we must abandon all foolish, short-term, PR-driven, empty and self-conscious celebrations of our own creativity, more appropriate to and becoming of a county the size of Rutland than a real nation. This perspective cannot be aided by the adolescent, craven, and nervous recruitment of non-Scots residents to the most culturally sensitive positions in the national arts. What is this, exactly? The *football*? Regardless of their expertise, how can *anyone* who has not lived here for some time – who does not know our complex history, who has no first-hand experience of the psychological makeup of our citizenry, who is not familiar with the work of our leading artists and writers – possibly react to our cultural biosphere in a way that will not caricature it, elide it, or reinvent the wheel? Yes, we were legally obliged to advertise these posts UK-wide – but we can now infer how negligible a knowledge of Scottish culture was in the interview process.

I propose that we end any further neurotic 'celebration' of our creativity. We need the direct appreciation of the arts, not some sentimental, reflexive, self-congratulatory meta-appreciation. We need the freedom to start *failing* a little, and to learn a modesty appropriate to our imminent international status. 'Celebrating our creativity' simply repeats our old nervous habit of selling ourselves back to ourselves, and is Kailyard 2.0. This is not helped by the Little Scotlanders in the academy, the government and the arts themselves who insist on either the democracy of talent, or surveying that talent at such a high degree of resolution that they see it flourishing everywhere. (For perspective: a Scottish body equivalent to the Royal Society of Literature in its selectivity would have thirty-odd members. *What* is it, precisely, that makes us so exceptionally talented that we would feel this to be an elitist outrage?) This leaves such genuine talent as we *do* have often left to fight its own way into the public mind. Again, the absence of any oversight from those best placed to provide it does nothing to help. In bringing some perspective, we remain grateful to England. Lord alone knows how long it would've taken me to read WS Graham without the meticulous advocacy of my Southron cousins, while my elders were still telling me to read Sydney Goodsir Smith. In that regard, we are still deeply ill-qualified to go it alone.

The longer we *see* each other acting like children, the longer trust will take to establish. But if we can learn to trust ourselves, and trust each other, create social structures where experts can meet as peers, and there concede and share our various creative expertise; if we can allow the ideas and art that emerge to be properly disseminated, exposed and corrected by an educated lay consensus – I believe Scotland can begin to dream the way it used to. The first step will be to destroy Creative Scotland's dysfunctional ant-heap (I could find no polite synonym for 'clusterfuck'), the product of a shocking SNP policy vacuum and a New Labour neo-managerialism incapable of understanding the difference between art and business. (Let me spell it out for those still confused: *investing in art has no guaranteed return. If it does, it isn't art.*) The second will be to take the adult decision of trusting its artists with art, its administrators with administration, its brokers with brokerage – and then make the almost unimaginable leap of simply trusting each other. Until then we will deserve our reputation as a nation of amateurs, who invest their precious and shrinking resources not in the creation and distribution of books, art, music, drama, not in the means by which the nation can dream, aspire, inspire – but in third-rate cookery programmes.

As I write, I note that the almost uniformly illiterate Creative Scotland Awards website is asking for nominations. Under 'Literature Awards', we read that 'Scotland is home to some of the most celebrated literary works in history, and continues to produce writers with skill, flare and the ability to communicate'. 'Flare' as in 'distress flare', we assume – of the kind now being fired from the restless graves of Dunbar, Lyndsay, Hume, Burns, Scott, MacDiarmid and Spark. The outcry is growing, but you can be certain of one thing: Creative Scotland's first thought will not be a reimagining, a rebirth or a reform – but a rebrand. We should not allow it.

JAMES ROBERTSON

I.

'The day after independence, nothing much will have changed.
It will be a normal day, the same as the days that went before it.'
  So the Big Man tells me.

'The day after independence, there will be weeping and
gnashing of teeth, for the land will have been cast into the outer
darkness.'
  So the Wee Folk tell me.

The Big Man tells me not to worry.
  The Wee Folk tell me to be feart, awfie feart.

What worries me about being told not to worry, is that it sounds
a little patronising, like being *excused* from thinking. 'Just put
your X in the right place and leave the rest to us.' And I worry
about voting for change only to find that there isn't much of it.
  What bugs me about being told to be feart, is that it sounds
like a threat. Am I being *warned* not to think? 'Just put your X in
the right place and you need never be fearful again.'
  Sorry. Not good enough. Thinking, by lots of people and on
a grand scale, is exactly what needs to happen in Scotland over
the next two years, and for a good while longer after that. In an
interview with BBC Scotland's Glen Campbell in April 2012, the
former leader of the Canadian Liberal Party Michael Ignatieff

made some useful, unhysterical observations. 'Everyone is watching Scotland... It's crucial that there's a proper national debate, so people look each other in the eye and say "What do I really want?" Politics doesn't often offer people that kind of wonderful moment of choice. This is a once-in-a-200-years opportunity'.

Aye, it is. And it's an opportunity – or it should be – not only to say 'Yes, please' or 'No, thanks' to a constitutional concept, but to go beyond the concept and make a maquette, or a series of them, showing what Scotland could look like in, say, ten, twenty and fifty years' time. Build your ideal – your *realistically* ideal – country from the available resources, including the human ones. Then debate whether that country can be better achieved through independence or through remaining part of the Union. Assuming that it's a destination most of us want to get to, will constitutional change help or hamper the journey to that country?

These maquettes – or if you want more detail, call them architectural models – will, obviously, have to be works of imagination, but they will be works of *informed* imagination, built by people with vision, skill and knowledge. It's only through that kind of combination – information and imagination – that this debate can break away from being a slagging match between parties already in entrenched positions, and offer the population as a whole a real choice. First, show us the country and nation that Scotland could be. Then decide the constitutional route by which we get there.

II.

For fifty years or thereabouts (most of my life, in other words) I've been broadly of the view that Scotland should once again be independent. (I've certainly never doubted the Scottish people's right of self-determination.) In a world full of independent countries and nations of all shapes and sizes, Scottish independence has never seemed to me an unrealistic or outlandish (interesting word) ambition. It's not been a driving force in my life, not made me want to enter politics or take up arms or man barricades, but it's part of how I think of the world. There are bigger issues facing humanity, but these are not contradicted or confounded, in my view, by wishing to see Scotland running its own affairs. Even those who think this scenario undesirable now concede that it is possible, although the scare stories (poverty, remoteness, smallness, lack of economic or military or intellectual clout) keep coming, mainly from the Right. The notion that Scotland, alone of European nations, is incapable of self-government is palpable nonsense.

Redundant too is the Left's old argument that Scottish independence as an objective was a diversion from the greater, higher goal of international equality and freedom for all people. It was an argument always selectively applied: some countries' liberation movements were deemed progressive because they were anti-imperialist and/or anti-capitalist. Others' (including Scotland's, and often it seemed *only* Scotland's) were regressive: not liberation struggles at all but bourgeois reactions to the stresses and failings of the capitalist system. But since the revolutions of 1989 – and more recently with the events of the Arab Spring – that rationale has vanished: one country's revolutionary experience may influence its neighbours, but nobody expects its people to wait patiently till everybody else is ready to throw off their chains.

Also gone, with the redefinition of New Labour as a centre-right party, is the guilty sense that Scottish socialists who dallied with Home Rule, let alone full-blown independence, were betraying their brothers and sisters south of the Border. In the words attributed to the late Jimmy Reid, 'It wasn't so much that I left Labour. I felt that they left me'. So in theory, at least, there should no longer be any obstacle – brought on by guilt or misplaced caution – to constructing a fully developed, coherent description of how independence could lead to an inclusive, democratic, egalitarian, culturally diverse, peaceful, ecologically responsible, economically sustainable society fit for purpose in the twenty-first century.

Yet there is. Here we are, two years out from the first occasion we've had to vote for or against independence *without* the complication of having to elect a government in either London or Edinburgh at the same time, and the word from the leaders of the political party whose *raison d'être* is independence is that, actually, it won't make a lot of difference. Eighty years it has taken, from the formation of the Scottish National Party (or three hundred and a few more if you start the clock from 1707), to get to a place where that same SNP, the party that has benefited most from the devolution settlement modelled by the Constitutional Convention it declined to join, can pop the divorce question to us. And what is it saying? Don't worry, life will carry on pretty much as it is.

We'll keep the monarchy. We won't even discuss how keeping the monarchy might get us off on the wrong foot. (Those architectural models, incidentally, really have to include an edifice labelled 'constitution for a twenty-first century Scottish democracy'.) We'll stick with the pound and let the Bank of England set our interest rates and borrowing levels. Honestly, you'll hardly feel a thing. Oh, and we'll somehow persuade NATO to remove its nuclear arsenal from our lochs and glens, but we'll still be *in* NATO. You can sleep soundly at night. Our justice system? What's wrong with it? It's Scottish, so in perfect working order. Our education system? Surely you're not questioning the quality of Scottish education?

I understand the difference between tactics and strategy. I understand about not frightening the horses – although actually I think it would be good to see a few wide-eyed sidelong glances and hear a nervous clattering of hooves. But to close down the big questions for fear of scaring off potential yes-voters with some big answers is no way to go about ushering in a new era – if that's what this is about, as surely it must be. Where are the maquettes, the architectural designs, the working models of a possible future? Where is the vision, the purpose, the meaning of it all? Where is the imagination?

Give us something to tell the next generation, and the one after that, that will make them feel proud of us. 'What did *you* do in the referendum, auld yin?' Give us a set of reasons – not pie-in-the-sky but genuine ideals and hopes we can strive to attain – that will drive us to the ballot-boxes saying 'This is the country I want'. Don't let those bairns, grown to middle age, stare dumbfounded at us and cry, 'You voted yes because you thought you'd be £500 better off? *That* was your reason?' Don't give them the opportunity to say, 'No wonder it all went so sour. You should have left well alone'. Because if we have the choice, as we will have, and opt for independence out of small-mindedness, or greed, or envy, or hatred, then we should, we really should, leave well alone, and make our calculations of what is possible for Scotland on a different scale. And if we make another choice, and vote for the Union out of fear, then we'll deserve all we will consequentially get.

'The enemies of Scottish nationalism are not the English,' declared Robert Bontine Cunninghame Graham in an address at Bannockburn in 1930, 'for they were ever a great and generous folk, quick to respond when justice calls. Our real enemies are among us, born without imagination'. Cunninghame Graham is worth investigating: an aristocrat and a socialist, a co-founder with Keir Hardie of both the Scottish Labour Party and the Independent Labour Party, and first President of the Scottish National Party. You could say he was full of contradictions and inconsistencies. Or you could say that he was consistently a true friend to Scotland. He was also, by the way, a great horseman, who neither tolerated the abuse of animals nor was frightened of frightening them.

III.

Three more quotations. They seem significant. They seem pertinent. Maybe they are, maybe they aren't.

Many years ago, I watched a TV documentary about a woman in Shetland who, young and unmarried, had single-handedly taken on the family croft when her parents died. She had worked that croft for decades. Now she was old, and could no longer manage all the tasks on her own. Neighbours and friends helped out. 'Don't you get frustrated that you can't do it all?' the interviewer asked – or something close to that. The reply has stuck with me ever since: 'Never resent growing old. It's an experience denied to many'. It's sound philosophy, for an individual or for a nation.

Edwin Morgan's poem 'King Billy' was published in his 1968 collection *The Second Life*. It concludes with these lines – lines that seem to look back, then turn and look forward:

> Go from the grave. The shrill flutes
> are silent, the march dispersed.
> Deplore what is to be deplored,
> and then find out the rest.

What are they saying, those lines? Perhaps that to go into the future you have to know your past, but you don't have to be trapped by it. Perhaps that there is always more to find out, and that we may be surprised by our prejudices and by our tolerances.

The third quotation comes from Thomas Masaryk, the founding father and first President of an independent Czechoslovakia. It is also the title of an address given by Neal Ascherson to the SNP's annual conference in Dunoon in 1986. That address is reprinted in Ascherson's book *Games With Shadows* (1988) and should be required reading for anyone who honestly and seriously asks the question 'What is independence for?' and wants honest and serious answers. Masaryk's advice to his people on the eve of their independence in 1918 was brief and to the point: 'Don't be afraid – and don't steal!'

What connects these three quotations, and the one from Cunninghame Graham too? That's interesting territory to explore. We have two years. But I know already that I like them a whole lot better than being told, on the one hand, that with independence nothing much will change, and on the other, that with independence I can expect to spend my days and nights in fear and trembling.

'Don't be afraid – and don't steal!' An individual, a nation, can go a long way guided by those moral imperatives.

SUHAYL SAADI

If there is to be independence, then in my view it ought to be profound and radical. To refer to the heraldry of our 'Pàrlamaid na h-Alba', I wish to see a brain, not a crown, above the Saltire.

There would be no point in swapping Mayfair for Morningside, the *Eastenders* theme tune for 'Flower of Scotland' or, God forbid, The Queen, for The Queen.

Aff wi the Croon! Aff wi aw croons… an coronets, tae!
Aff with aw thon bally-hoo!
Bit pray, who, in the nem ae Wullie Wally, Rabbie Bruce an
     Joahn Maxton
Who the fuck ur yoo?

To achieve sufficient grounding, it is recommended that at this point one listens to Kazi Nazrul Islam, Faiz Ahmed Faiz and Tom Leonard. By inclination I am not a nationalist. I find the panoply – flags, national anthems – at best constructed and at worst tribal, supremacist and exclusive. I would rather watch *Doris The Builder*. However, signifiers change over time. Think of the flag of Palestinian warrior saint George of Lod, or even the dyspractic Union Jack and the cultural polyvalence of the Mods. Those at the centre are what they are, the rest of us are international adaptor plugs – we modulate. The human condition is quantum.

Now you see me,   now you see me,   now you see me,

But who, in the name of Saint Columba, Yahya Knox and Lobey Dosser am I to pontificate on other people's lives, jobs, futures? If the economics isn't feasible, then independence is a dead haggis. Will the economics work? It might, but one would need to be vigilant for the paladins of empire who tend to sow cartographical and other seeds of destruction as they take their grudging leave – witness, Kashmir, Palestine/Israel, Northern Ireland. That ought not to terrify or detain us, but it ought to render unto us a diamond-hard vigilance.

Social class is the grouse in the sitting-room. Over the past 300 years, enough Scottish soldiers have died and killed, and maimed and been maimed in foreign fields. There is a shither of discomfort with kilts and bagpipes. Those who sport full tribal High Street costume tend to be six-foot-two rugby-playing public schoolboys named 'Andrew, Son-of-Farquhar MacTavish-Sinclair'. Or to put it another way, phenomenologically speaking, perhaps there really is nothing underneath.

Wealth distribution is the single most important determinant of everything. To quote from Benjamin Disraeli's iconic 1845 novel, *Sybil, or The Two Nations*:

> 'Two nations; between whom there is no intercourse and no sympathy; who are as ignorant of each other's habits, thoughts, and feelings, as if they were dwellers in different zones, or inhabitants of different planets; who are formed by a different breeding, are fed by a different food, are ordered by different manners, and are not governed by the same laws.' 'You speak of —' said Egremont, hesitantly. 'THE RICH AND THE POOR.'

In contemporary Britain, too, the real border runs not between the Solway and the Tweed, but through the Antonine Wall of Drumchapel/Bearsden. I hear that outside of London and the south-east, Scotland is the biggest wealth generator in the UK. Yet it is claimed that around one in five Scots is functionally illiterate. If you are illiterate, you are rammed like a rivet into the side of the ship and when the ship goes down, so do you.

Balkanisation is a worrying tendency. But in the absence of a global anarchist, clarsach-strumming commune, the nation-state, with all its inherent paradoxes and flamboyant nonsense, currently seems to be the only possible bulwark. This dialectical axis has been appropriated by – or rather, conveniently delivered to – the Extreme Right, so that the contemporary battle-lines run between transnational corporate capitalism and xenophobic chauvinism. Where the organised Left used to be, there is a black hole. Words, yes, but you cannot eat words, you can only spit them out. Yet perhaps, somewhere beyond the event horizon, something now is rising.

Divide-and-rule is the modus operandum of empire; it must not be a feature of the new Scotland. Cheap labour, domestically and abroad, is used to undercut wages and employment and facilitates the massive and distorting accumulation of capital by the very few on which all of it is premised. Yet immigrants and their descendents create wealth and jobs (and much else). The Left must resolve this dilemma of resisting both dead-end xenophobia and the hegemonic power of international capital.

Participatory democracy might reduce the tendency towards plutocracy, though one worries about majoritarian tribalism (Scotland is a profoundly tribal society and not just in the obvious ways – another area of tacit denial) and Tammany Hall, so there would need to be strong checks and balances built in. It would be difficult to achieve any of this while in the belly of the EU/WTO whale, which is driven not by egalitarianism or liberty but by neo-liberalism. Either you have democracy, or you don't. Are there allies locally with which Scotland could form a northern version of the contemporary South American macro-economic united front? Norway? Post-2008 Iceland? But first, let us show ideologically driven cartels like News International the big welly-boot. Then, let us exit the WTO and the EU and impose import controls. Then, and only then, will manufacturing have a chance better than that of a field-mouse in Hell. Then, and only then, will Scotland be truly independent.

If such a configuration were realistic for the area that is currently Great Britain – economic redistribution, participatory democracy, proper investment in 'blue sky' ideas, inventions and entrepreneurialism, no monarchy/aristocracy, no NATO, no nukes and compulsory LSD for book reviewers – I would be fine with England, Scotland and Wales remaining one country; I believe in a united Ireland (though ideally, one without *Riverdance*). The much-vaunted UK arms industry is hugely subsidised by the UK taxpayer and creates and sustains fewer jobs than it claims. As with the economy as a whole, the risk is socialised, the profits, privatised via tax havens. It generates grand corruption of the body politic and the blowback is immense. If the concept of Scottish Independence in the twenty-first century is to mean anything, it ought to mean something different from the dominant paradigm – it would need to be the end of Kali Yuga!

It seems clear, however, that the profoundly imperialist United Kingdom will never change and that there is no significant mass movement among the working classes – us – for systemic economic change within the UK. Wall Street and the war machine are mosquitoes and malaria on the banks of the Thames, and are emblematic of a durbar empire reduced to a plantation of clinker and cocaine.

Now, in the manner of medieval court jesters, let us stand on our heads.

Language is the universe. Public Relations (aka 'comms', aka propaganda) dominates our brave new lives. It requires constant mental adroitness to combat the appropriation of the collective imagination; it now is deemed abnormal to refuse to be brainwashed. Perhaps then, especially if one is not producing but only consuming, democracy has come to subsist in the freedom merely to choose one's own, peculiar form of 'schizophrenia', one's own, specific, individuated brand of alienation. Yet even this seems determined by the agents of influence of the 'permanent government', the plutonium of the corporate security plexus. We imagine that we are free and strong, yet like Dr Gulliver, we are held down by a thousand fine threads.

Another example of the demise of rationalism is the resurrection of the Victorian 'syndrome', of multi-system complexes with no measurable parameters. These 'pain and exhaustion' syndromes elicit high profile, aggressive (and, ironically, energetic) entitlement group campaigning. And Psychiatry adds to the confusion, with brand-new 'diseases', ratified, codified and beatified by the World Health Organisation, with names like 'Narcissistic Personality Disorder' or 'Adjustment Disorder'. This is politics as pathology. Does no-one read Huxley or Orwell any more? Is it no longer permissible to say and believe *that it is not we, but the system that is fucked and that is fucking us* and that we are mad as hell and aren't going to take this any more? We see the banal corollary of this sublimation of unhappiness in pharmacological form in the West of Scotland, where a not insubstantial proportion of the population imbibes (prescribed or otherwise) analgesia as a matter of course, like lumps of sugar or casters of salt. Opium is the religion of the people.

And on religion, no more pandering, please, to supremacist, bigoted, homophobic lobbies. Scotland should be a systemically secular entity. Shared campuses ought logically to lead to non-denominational schooling; once and for all, let's stop the separation of our children. But no more sacrificing quality for platitude, no more lowering of standards to generate falsely inflated results. Learn this (something our recent ancestors knew very well): learning, expanding the compass of one's mind and reality, is bloody difficult and often, especially at the start, is frustratingly tedious. But that is the only way to learn. In order to stand on the shoulders of giants, one first must clamber up their gnarled bodies and drink their sweat and piss.

Speaking of which...

It is clear to me that much contemporary literature in Scotland possesses distinct methodological features and a non-insular vitality which, after around 35 years, if one is living in this breezy country, one perhaps tends to take for granted but which one realises (with a thud) is distinct when one voyages through space, time, code and social class, to literary events in, say, the south of England. And I am convinced that on some barely conscious level, the discourses mediated by these features have contributed towards the shaping of attitudes in Scotland over the past few decades.

There has been cultivated, especially among the brown sons and daughters of empire who think His Master's Thoughts and speak with His Master's Voice (Oxbridge and SOAS, I salute thee!), a perpetual hankering for Edwardian English, a form of iteration and cogitation which has been constructed in our public spaces as normative and also indicative, in the quasi-Darwinian sense, of cultural maturity. One's over-riding impression, from reading many novels by English authors, is the dislocation between a specific socio-economic subset within the meta-metropolis of London and the rest of England (let alone Scotland, Wales, Ireland et al) – the relentless, yet seemingly unquestioned, tendency towards the centralisation of the imagination.

It is a function of empire that different subaltern groupings come to maintain themselves in exclusive dualistic and dependent relationships with the imperial centre, so that they remain mutually incomprehensible. Are we to have only cartelised publishing houses that churn out yet more colonial and baronial fiction, that cultivate a market for more of the same? Whither, then, independence?

Cynical reviewers of this book will tremble with rage and will intone:

Where are the heroes
Who draw the thistle across their eyes
And their souls from pitchers of slate-grey dawn?

Where are the men of steel and iron,
The entrepreneurs of the Rampant Lion?

Am I a Don Quixote, a seeker of utopias? Utopia tends to get broken on the wheel of human imperfection. Perhaps that is why I quite like risking incompetence of syntax on the point of a lance.

If we were to be transported back to Ancient Egypt in 2,000 BCE and were to suggest to the people of the Nile that one day, there would be no pharaoh, that slavery would have been abolished, that workers would have rights and that Isis was just a pretty woman with a profitable line in mascara, they too would have laughed, made sarcastic jokes and labelled one mad, incompetent and hopelessly immature. The sun set remarkably quickly, equatorial-style, on the British Empire. Yet we live now in the slippery age of liberal neo-imperium: instead of gin and pith helmets, we have NGOs.

What I am calling for, then, is a revolution in the head as well as in the exchequer. And revolutions tend to be carried on the backs of donkeys.

One does not have to be an acolyte of Whig histories to see the pattern of the song repeating as though it were a meme in a folk-tale carried in moonlight on the backs of singing donkeys across different terrains, across continents of time. Well, once again, it seems, the donkey has reached Scotland. But who is riding, and who singing?

You see – and at the risk of leaping once more upon my hobby-horse and riding it to Partick Cross – I think that there is a coffin which is lodged firmly and comfortably in a cartel warehouse in London whose contents must be approved by the (outsourced) Cartel of Coffins and which must never be opened, for fear that it bursts open and releases the Blue-eyed Banshee. It is sealed by means of a gleaming latch in which one can see one's own face.

MIKE SMALL

Until the referendum we are in a liminal land, neither here nor there, roamin' in the gloaming. Depending on your aspirations, or fears, we are stuck between here and the promised land, or some kind of neo-Darien hell. The choice is simple: a culturally inspired Alba or an economically desperate Albania: Yes or No. We are waiting to see what we decide. Will we 'Vote No for Scotland's future!' as one confused Togetherite declared at the No campaign launch, or – as Pixar's trailer for *Brave* exhorts – 'Decide our own destiny'?

In Liminal Land one group of politicians is accused of spreading false hope while another spreads doubt and fear. But both campaigns have problems with this attempt to project forward to some imagined future, because while they can play safe to respective dreams or anxieties, it's in today's here and now that Britain is falling apart. This collapse of cultural icons, financial security, institutional stability and political credibility could either play into the hands of those attempting to encourage a sense of anxiety amongst voters – or reveal the truth that there isn't any longer a 'Britain' to remain part of.

Dealing with the here and now is problematic for both campaigns. For No it is a disastrous confirmation not just that the coalition government is deeply unpopular but that the institutions they represent are failing, and failing because of two decades' worth of shared policy focus. Not only policies have failed but the belief systems that underpin them.

For the Yes campaign, Britain's shuddering malfunction may

force them to outline details of alternatives, something everyone has been reluctant to do. If the banks are run by crooks – what does this mean? If Britain has no constitution that can protect you, what can be done about that? How do you write a bill of rights? What does decentralised public control look like?

Here are three motifs of the liminal political scene which the Yes campaign should exploit to turn a negative campaign against independence into a transformative movement for it.

Failed Elite Rule

The banking crisis is yet another disgrace for the country's governing elites, but it shouldn't be seen in isolation. Seamus Milne has written of the City's unmuzzled power and the cumulative impact of a value-free British politics: 'The new revelation of corruption comes after the exposure of the deception of the Iraq war, fraud in parliament and the police, the criminality of a media mafia and the devastating failure of the banks four years ago. It could of course happen only in a private-dominated financial sector, and makes a nonsense of the bankrupt free-market ideology that still holds sway in public life' (*Guardian*, 3 July 2012).

We now inhabit a time when no-one really trusts the logic of Westminster politicians, however much everyday life, and the routines of daily media, oblige us to pretend otherwise. A daily news bulletin contains segments – news, business, sport. It is increasingly difficult to disentangle the three. But the cheerleader-style reporting of the business section increasingly grates as late-capitalism unfolds in all its gory, over-paid excess. Fine and tolerated (perhaps) while we were all riding high on the hog of housing boom and fuller employment, but scarcely credible, morally or practically, whilst youth unemployment rockets and the Tory-Liberal austerity measures and 'welfare reforms' hit home. Fred the Shred and Bob Diamond may be the happy couple who give birth to the independent child with aspirations for better, but Alistair Darling and George Osborne are the 'light touch' midwives.

The sheen has come off as the palpable failure of elite rule hits home: from failure to manage, acknowledge or respond to the banking crisis; to the inability to legislate or censor the out-of-control media exposed by the Leveson Inquiry. At its heart the referendum offers the prospect of power to change beyond constitutional paternalism. As one wag put it when firearms legislation was being proposed at Holyrood, 'with devolution you get to ban air-rifles, with independence you can cancel Trident'.

Groups like Vote for a Change are mushrooming and likely to reinforce the idea of a failed political class mired in corruption, back-handers and moat expenses. As the recession bites, memories will remain warm of politicians living in an alternate world. Holyrood has its own problems, and is not immune from petty dishonesty, but for practical reasons it isn't swamped with the same association of base venality that now dogs Westminster. It's not a gigantic leap to suggest that not only the political classes need disbanded, but the British State itself. The death of Ian Tomlinson in 2009, the growth of a surveillance culture, the collapse of credibility of the Metropolitan Police – all these should be a focus of analysis. All that would be required would be some sense of what might be better.

Networked Change

A new phenomena is driving this collapse in credibility, with a power of exposure and collaboration which should be focused and encouraged. So far this phenomena has been pigeon-holed as 'Cyber Nats' but in fact it's a whole society online and a whole civic society organising.

Across Britain groups like Uncut and internationally Occupy have proved the effectiveness of the network, breathing new life into the alter-globalisation movement, said to be stalled after the big set-piece demos of Seattle, Genoa, London and Gleneagles. There's a Scottish dimension to this. As well as the mushrooming of the Scottish blogosphere as antidote to the mainstream media there is a slew of new, positive cultural projects that offer the potential to engage a far wider section of people than the already committed and the already engaged politicos.

Projects like the National Collective ('join, create, collaborate') [nationalcollective.com], We Are Northern Lights [wearenorthernlights.com], KILTR ('one clan many cultures') [www.kiltr.com] the Leith based photo-journal Blipfoto [www.blipfoto.com] and the Scottish Album of the Year Awards [sayaward.com]. These initiatives offer not just a cultural dimension to the network but a blueprint and a reflection of the self-determination model. They are driven by and for *participation* in ways that seem increasingly, markedly different from the British experience, characterised by the Diamond Jubilee pageant of feudalism, resistance to change of the House of Lords, an unaccountable Metropolitan police force and a centralising tendency that is as acute as it is both cultural and political.

Nor is the reach of these projects confined to cultured 'luvvies' or the already-committed online hardcore. We've just seen the transformation of Scottish football, realised almost entirely through Twitter and key fan sites: Rangers Tax Case, Pie and Bovril and Scotzine to name just three. Whatever you think of the rights and wrongs of the Rangers liquidation fiasco, there is no doubt SPL chairmen would have quite happily connived to retain or return Newco Rangers back to the top flight if not for a networked resistance of ordinary fans. A right royal institution of the union has been brought down before our eyes by united action across Scotland. This is a sizeable result by any standards, and one achieved by a network without any single identifiable leadership. This is key. Perhaps the independence movement's greatest asset is also its weakest point: a total focus on one individual. If one lesson can be learnt from these networked movements, it is that strength comes from the width of the net. Resilience comes from the model of many speaking to many, not the model of one to many.

Just Say No

A few thoughts on negativity – relentless, hopeless, and mindless. The difficulty the No campaign has is that its defining argument is about security and Britain's place in the world. Both stem from and reinforce a feeling of decline and threat, and both move the argument onto territory where the No campaign doesn't want to be. On foreign policy the endless scaremongering about immigration, terrorism, consulates and military employment recur again and again. But each of these draws the issues back to uncomfortable ground. Isn't most terrorism we're talking about the result of Britain's disastrous botched illegal wars in Iraq and Afghanistan? Isn't immigration a completely different issue north and south of the border? Are we really to believe that in the twenty-first century the only jobs we have to offer our young men are building ships and arms for an imaginary Cold War?

Whilst the will may be there for a positive case for the union, it remains elusive. It oscillates from the banal to the ridiculous. If you want to paint your face with a Union Jack, listen to the Archers and genuflect at the Queen, be my guest. None of that is threatened by your parliament being able to make decisions.

The relentless and enduring negativity of the Better Together campaign and its unconscious lackeys in the Anglo-British media will have an impact. 'Would you move house in a hurricane?' asked one dark tweet. It neatly shifted the ground from one of bad decisions, a culture of unremitting greed and a failure of leadership and values, to one suggesting the financial crisis was simply a force of nature.

Some or all of this may stick. People may be duped, confidence may falter, but historical slide suggests otherwise. The very institutions that could hold Britain together as an idea have been picked apart, privatised, sold-off or dismantled by two decades of neo-liberal politicians who can hardly now appeal to the NHS, the Post Office or a common media voice as indicators of a common future, never mind a shared past. The lesson for the No campaign team: if you place so little value in these institutions then don't rely on them to tell your political story.

Churnalists and unionist spinners have decided already. The Scots won't vote for independence in 2014. It won't happen. It can't happen. We've heard this before. We heard it before the devolution vote. We heard it only weeks before the SNP landslide in 2011 when 'arc of insolvency' jibes rang harsh in the ears of independence campaigners. Now we hear that the Eurocrisis will have the same chilling effect.

But collapsonomics and the shifting sands of relations between global and local, individual and community, self and identity, culture and technology can unleash unexpected results. A fractured, discredited print media, a London government that appears like a throwback to the Edwardian era, and the catastrophic failure of the Labour Party to create a political narrative are combining. All this on top of twenty years of cultural renewal and a growing sense of, if not confidence, declining self-hatred. In a post-ideological world, against the backdrop of Britain in perpetual crisis, the idea of starting a nation 'afresh' may seem compelling.

What was once impregnable, deeply certain, now seems affected by the same precarity as the rest our existence. As Tom Nairn writes in *After Britain* (2000):

> The Constitution of old England-Britain once stood like a mighty dam, preserving its subjects from such a fate; nowadays, leaking on all sides, it merely guides them to the appropriate slope or exit. Blairism has

reformed just enough to destabilise everything, and to make a reconsolidation of the once-sacred earth of British Sovereignty impossible. As if panicked by this realisation, his government has then begun to run round in circles groaning that enough is enough, and that well must now be left alone. The trouble is that everything is now broken – at least in the sense of being questioned, uncertain, a bit ridiculous, lacking in conviction, up for grabs, floundering, demoralised and worried about the future.

That was more than a decade ago. Figures such as Alastair Darling, Charles Kennedy and Blair are yesterday's men, indelibly tainted by yesterday's failures. You can almost feel the hand of history on Tony's shoulder once again.

GERDA STEVENSON

Another day, and another preview under the belt – Communicado Theatre Company's *Tam O' Shanter* at Assembly, on the Edinburgh Fringe. But, for me, not just another preview. It was something special today, because the last time I performed in the wonderful arena of the Assembly Hall, at the top of the Mound, was some thirty years ago in Sir David Lindsay's revolutionary, and now rarely produced, *Ane Pleasant Satyre of the Thrie Estaitis.* Among the fine cast were Andrew Cruickshank and Robert Urquhart, directed by my old friend Tom Fleming, then Artistic Director of the Scottish Theatre Company. Another era.

Scotland's theatre tradition is an unusual one. It started with a bang in the mid-sixteenth century, and resumed after a silence of centuries. Lindsay's astonishingly modern epic is a major political drama challenging the injustices wreaked by the pre-Reformation controlling powers of Scottish society, including the deeply corrupt (Catholic) church. It's written in gorgeously rich old Scots, full of French resonances, and a Chaucerian earthiness – prudes might call it 'filthy' today. Seen at the time as heresy, copies were publicly burned; it's lucky the text survived. Then came the fierce, cold blast of the Reformation, in some respects a force for democratisation, but nevertheless fundamentalist, with its Presbyterian anti-art agenda. This form of Protestant religion had, I believe, a spiritually crippling impact on Scottish culture, a legacy still apparent, particularly in the West Highlands and Islands. Presbyterianism is burned into our nation's collective subconscious.

I was reminded of this in a Donegal supermarket a couple of years ago, when the woman at the check-out, hearing my accent, asked where I was from. 'Scotland,' I told her, 'I'm reading at the poetry festival.' 'Oh, you're a poet! Now isn't that just grand!' she enthused. I can't imagine such an exchange at a Scottish supermarket check-out!

In spite of this history, I think contemporary Scotland increasingly believes in the importance of art – including theatre – to all of its citizens. And the iconoclastic spirit of *The Thrie Estaitis* still survives, thanks to the pioneering Tyrone Guthrie, who, in 1948, exhumed Lindsay's script from the dust of ages and mounted a production of a shortened version (cleaned up – the Lord Chamberlain's censorship prevailing then) at the Edinburgh Festival.

Scotland's modern theatre tradition has roots reaching back through centuries to that great play – Ena Lamont Stewart's *Men Should Weep* from Glasgow's Unity Players, John McGrath's 7:84 Theatre Company with its seminal *The Cheviot, The Stag And The Black, Black Oil*, and the National Theatre of Scotland's *Black Watch* by Gregory Burke. While politics hasn't necessarily defined its identity, social and political themes have been central to Scottish theatre for decades.

What's the appetite for such work? How representative of our audience is such content and preoccupation? How political is the average Scot? According to opinion polls, most Scots want universal public services. Which is why Scotland isn't a stronghold of the British Conservative party. We prize our National Health Service, our education system, and try to cling on to them. Unlike our neighbours across the border, we have free personal care for the elderly, and our university students don't pay tuition fees. Ask Scots if they want to undo Margaret Thatcher's work and re-nationalise the railways, I reckon they'd respond with an overwhelming Yes. There's evidence that Scots are predisposed to communality. There are theories about this – that it's the legacy of our ancient clan system; that our Kings and Queens were always of Scots, not of Scot*land*. What matters to us is the community of people. Interesting, in this context, to contemplate that Gaelic has no verb 'to own'.

Awareness of our planet's multiplicity of languages and cultures has become heightened with the advent of the internet. Scottish dramatists increasingly employ the true voices of their characters. We're comfortable with foreign films and subtitles. We have public debates in Scotland about our languages, over the importance of nurturing Scots and Gaelic. There's an appetite for plays written in Scots, the best known being translations of classics, particularly Molière and Goldoni. The late Edwin Morgan created scintillating Scots translations, directly from the French. I was fortunate to play the title role in his *Phaedra*, and also took part in the original production of Liz Lochhead's superb version of *Tartuffe*. Plays in Scots are a vibrant part of our theatre tradition, and draw big audiences.

Over the last decade, a unique development in Scottish theatre has established a home for new writing, at Oran Mor in Glasgow – *A Play, a Pie and a Pint* lunchtime theatre, produced by David MacLennan, with an astonishing output of over 40 new plays per annum. There's a big energy in our small nation's contemporary theatre. And, having sat on two separate committees campaigning for it, I'm glad to see the establishment, at last, of the National Theatre of Scotland.

We have a long, rich and internationally recognised literary tradition, particularly in poetry and prose. Many authors, including excellent playwrights, live and work here, some known beyond our borders. It's not quite the same for the acting community – one or two stars have homes in Scotland, but most well-known Scottish actors live in London, New York or Los Angeles, the nerve centres of celebrity. Although I trained in London (where I've also lived and worked), I'm rooted in Scotland. I'm excited by the rich professional theatre we're creating here. An artistic director of a Scottish theatre company, interviewed recently about leaving to take up another artistic directorship in England, commented 'as you go higher up the career ladder, the opportunities to work on the kind of scale I'll be able to work on, with the kind of profile, get fewer and fewer. It's really hard in Scotland to say, "Well, where do you go next?"' That view, still prevalent, though less so than before, implies that Scottish theatre is intrinsically second-rate. Of course, it's hugely beneficial to work in new places, get out of your comfort zone, discover new influences – but I wouldn't choose to do so for the reason quoted.

Virtually all the richly diverse professional theatre in Scotland today wouldn't exist without government investment. Business sponsors have their own needs in targeting a market, an agenda running counter to the artist's. Unusual or challenging art will rarely be supported from that constituency. If we had to rely on private sponsorship, we'd see nothing but West End musicals on our stages. (Don't get me wrong – I love big musicals!) And they'd be confined to the cities. The kind of theatre that's being created in Scotland, performing in cities and rural areas, wouldn't happen, and you'd have a de-professionalised, dormant theatre workforce, reliant on teaching in colleges and universities to earn a crust, or, at worst, unemployed. Nothing wrong with teaching, of course. But a group of students isn't the same as a professional company. And, anyway, in the long-run, why study theatre if there are hardly any professional companies left to employ graduates? Without government investment, we wouldn't have live professional theatre out there, producing new writing, the work of skilled practitioners, questioning, breaking boundaries. This bleak scenario more or less describes the status quo of contemporary theatre in the USA.

Of course, there's a role for non-state funding – Scottish theatre organisations are supported by individual trusts and some business partners – but most of our theatre companies (almost all registered charities limited by guarantee) rely on public funds. It depends on whether you believe in the spiritually civilising force of art as fundamental to a nation's well-being. If you do, then your government makes provision for it.

How does our vision reach out across borders? Creative Scotland (the absurdly, and confusingly, rebranded Scottish Arts Council) has prioritised international touring, exchanges and connections. There's a public perception that working in the Big Apple or the Big Smoke *de facto* ensures future funding and future success. While this can be the case, it's also true that cultures don't always easily transfer. I can think of real hits in Scotland that haven't been received well in London.

Nor can one say categorically that international touring has financial benefits (other than strengthening future applications to funding bodies). I recently discovered the reality of such exportation. I toured my play *Federer Versus Murray* to New York earlier in 2012, and found the surreal visa application process to be costly, requiring an American lawyer to navigate the labyrinthine bureaucracy. Everyone who's experienced it knows it's one of the most time-consuming, stress-inducing administrative obstacle courses you'll encounter. In spite of the Scottish Government's efforts to export its nation's culture to America during the annual *Scotland Week*, the US government is hardly holding its breath to receive its Scottish guests.

Another pressure, marching across every border, is the Stalker of Marketing: art must now be based on *brands*, the big idea, the theme that sells. I doubt that Chekov or Beckett ever sat down and thought: 'What's the BIG IDEA I can sell?' Of course, events in the world do inform artists' creativity, and so they should. But the prevailing celebrity and merchandise culture is a disease, a killer of art – death to the imagination, about nothing that's important or of any value, although it makes fortunes.

The celebrity cult is a conundrum. Celebrity artists are hugely valued in Scotland (as everywhere), yet, although they've usually developed their skills through commitment to their art, professional art is generally seen by Scots as an indulgence, not 'real' work, and – particularly by bureaucrats – as risky. But most artists I know have developed remarkable skills in responsible, reliable, shoe-string frugality. It's sickeningly ironic that under the prevailing business culture, bureaucratic organisations don't trust artists – a bit rich when we consider the recent disaster in the global financial sector, where business plans are supposed to have been the safety net.

In an economy driven by profit and competition, which has introduced business models into all its structures, the arts are problematic. By its very nature, art is indefinable, non-quantifiable. It doesn't respond to measurement by such pitifully unimaginative limitations. You can't assess a nation's spiritual wealth in terms of profit. Robert Owen, successful capitalist, iconoclast and social reformer, might have something to contribute on this subject, were he alive today. He certainly believed, early in his career as a mill owner at New Lanark during the 1800s, that the arts were fundamental to the health of his workforce. He provided education, daily dancing and music classes for all his workers and their children, set up infant childcare, and established many revolutionary social measures to enhance their welfare. He always said that music and dance were central to his philosophy of social reform. Businessmen during this early period of the industrial revolution, when slave labour in Britain's cotton mills was rife, were astonished to discover that Owen's New Lanark enterprise was the most profitable in Europe, and crime was negligible among his workforce. Perhaps some Owenite practices should be introduced in British schools, rather than Thatcherite Business Studies.

So where's Scotland heading? What do we see within our borders, and beyond? The approaching referendum on Scottish independence gives us an opportunity to ask ourselves what kind of society we wish to be. A chance to put our heads together creatively, and dare to produce a vision from the mire we're all wading through – the swamp of sinking aspirations, social deprivation and hardship, an unpardonable mess created by the globally rampant, criminally incompetent, rapacious, morally corrupt, tax-avoiding, bonus-grabbing, controlling financial sector. Do we want to be responsible, democratic, creative, caring citizens, respecting our environment, represented by a government that will ensure we can be just that? It won't happen if we're led by the kind of team currently in charge at Westminster. We'll have no public services left if we leave it to them.

Sometimes I think about Shakespeare's line in *Macbeth*, when Ross, referring to Scotland says: 'Alas, poor country, almost afraid to know itself'. I'd say there's a collective psychological truth in that line. And there's an energy in Scottish theatre that's currently exploring such territory: David Greig's *Dunsinane* responds in some ways to Ross's statement. The plays we see at Oran Mor in Glasgow are packed with ideas, full of vibrantly relevant debate and imagination.

One of the things I love about Scotland – probably something to do with the inevitable intimacy of a small country – is the way the arts cross-fertilise: painters, poets, musicians, songwriters, novelists, dancers, playwrights and film-makers (not all of them Scots, thank goodness – people of various cultural backgrounds and nationalities), connect with one another, making for vibrant interaction.

Rabindranath Tagore, the great Bengali poet wrote in 1940, and I agree with him: 'Love is kindred to art – it is inexplicable. There are other factors of life, which are visitors that come and go. Art is the guest that comes and remains. The others may be important, but art is inevitable.'

CHRISTOPHER WHYTE

I have never had any waverings about support for Scottish independence. Even four decades ago, I would have voted 'yes' without hesitation. Behind that lies a conscious, willing assumption of difference, as well as an impatience with discourses of victimhood, and a determination to move beyond victim positions, of whatever nature. What matters is, not complaining about what was done to us, but working out what it is up to us to do. I am convinced that writers, as well as intellectuals and creative people generally, invariably have their work mapped out for them. The welfare of the society where they belong is determined, at least in part, by how far they succeed in identifying that work, and carrying it out.

My own relation to Scottish society is marked by marginality of two specific kinds. If it would be foolish to claim that this offers me a privileged insight, it certainly influences the way I look at Scotland. On the one hand, at at least two points in my life, I have made a deliberate choice to live outside of Scotland, surrounding myself with another language and culture, in which I immersed myself. First came Italy, at the age of twenty, and then, aged fifty-two, Hungary and, more broadly, central Europe. Before the latter, for about a decade, Catalunya, irreparably bilingual, characterised by its cultural and economic dynamism, offered an idea of what a smaller nation might achieve. On the other, I grew up as Glaswegian as Glaswegian can be, in the West End of the city, educated by Jesuits and attending the mass in Latin, with an innate sense of otherness, of difference from canonical notions of being Scottish. This feeling of being different typifies many who have their origins in the city.

I wish an independent Scotland well. What follows partakes of the nature of good wishes. These are the things I would hope for in a country which was entirely self-governing – altruistically, not from any expectation that these developments might first and foremost benefit me.

My feeling is that Scotland's is a powerfully shame-based culture. Shaming is pervasive. It is something Scottish people do to one another, so that nobody will step out of line, so as to preserve a reassuring lowest common denominator, an unhelpful, destructive and illusory sameness, which is one meaning of 'identity'. Precisely because shame is so hard to talk about, bringing the shaming into consciousness is highly problematic. Shaming is always in the interests of a group or groups. It benefits someone in ways that are expertly camouflaged and, consequently, tricky to put a stop to. Uncovering agency in Scotland's history over the last three to four centuries will be impossible until victim positions are relinquished. The uprooting of the Gaelic-speaking peasantry, the savagery with which industrialisation came about and the persisting levels of poverty in Strathclyde are not ills inflicted from outside. They reflect dynamics of interaction between groups and interests based in Scotland. Describing what happened does not have to be primarily about apportioning blame. It can be done with detachment and objectivity.

Part, but only a part, of the shaming concerns sexuality. Wide-ranging affirmations are not always helpful. Nonetheless I am tempted to assert that, at some point in the past, Scottish people were robbed of their sexuality. Fear, even terror, of sexuality and everything connected with it is rife and, again, very difficult to bring into the light. I have the distinct impression that European cultures exist where this is not the case, or not to such a damaging extent. The phenomenon must be linked to the brands of Christianity practised within Scotland, and to the peculiar osmosis these engage in, the tendency of bodies claiming they are poles apart to assimilate, to come increasingly to resemble one another. Shame about sexuality has made things particularly difficult for women who, in Scotland, have been forced to masculinise in unconstructive ways. It has also affected the treatment of children, because they are the products of sexual activity (it feels stupid to have to point this out) and also, instinctively, shameless, at least until somebody interferes.

Public apologies need to be made. I belong to a generation of adults in whose schooling physical beating, or the threat of it, played an inordinate and determining role. Maybe this does not happen any more. But it still lives on, inside me. It will not go away until the enormity of what went on is fully acknowledged and some sort of reparation – on the simplest level, an apology – is offered. Several years ago, during a psychotherapy session, the issue of sexual abuse of children arose. Visibly distressed and perturbed, the therapist said: 'In Scotland, this is a hidden Holocaust'. Children are abused in every society we know about. Does shame about sexuality, and fear of it, make facing that abuse (note, I merely write 'facing', not 'healing') exceptionally difficult? My own fantasy (must it remain a fantasy?) is that one day Scotland's First Minister, be it a man or a woman, will appear on national television in order to apologise, not just to children being abused right now, but to all the adults this happened to, and whom our society failed to protect. Undertakings of this nature could only make things better. For everyone.

You can argue that, between 1880 and 1930, the major event in Scottish history was immigration from Ireland. Here, too, apologies need to be made and responsibilities assumed, also retrospectively. Would anyone claim that institutionalised discrimination against the immigrants and their offspring was less than endemic in Scottish society throughout the twentieth century? Whatever the situation may be now, until people accept that this happened, the effects will simply refuse to vanish. The picture is far from entirely bleak. Separate, state-funded education ensured that those suffering discrimination had access to protected areas within society, and were encouraged to maintain their difference from the putative majority, in religion, language and culture, for as long as they wanted – if needed, then forever. That was a success story. It explains why I personally cannot, in conscience, fail to be in favour of specific educational provision for those Muslims who want it, provided everyone in that community enjoys the same rights, and assumes the same civic responsibilities, as the rest of Scotland's inhabitants. The presence in our midst of communities of Asian origin cannot be anything but a blessing, in the longer run.

Perhaps what I am hoping for, not just on a symbolic level, is that those living in an independent Scotland can prove willing to face their dark side, which would mean an honest settling of accounts with the past. Our past is never over, never finished, we add to it and revise it in continuation. It is a mistake to subscribe to over-simplistic concepts of how past and present interact. Moreover, however afraid we may be of the darkness we carry inside us, and also inhabit, it can be the location of our most fruitful potential. We require darkness in order to rest effectively. The womb in which the foetus grows is dark. It is where those parts of us which we refuse to own are banished, or take refuge. Where our unconscious projections accumulate. We need to take a look at them and turn them into friends, while not kidding ourselves about the limits within which this can be achieved.

Moving out of victimhood means we no longer concentrate on what the rest of the world, on what outsiders (who may well be identified in our own midst) are said to have taken from us, or perpetrated. The unavoidable bottom line is managing Scotland and its resources effectively. Starting to reverse the ecological disaster represented by the Highlands, our very own wilderness, or garbage heap. Confronting the scandal of inequitable land ownership. Deciding that levels of poverty in the urbanised central belt are not merely unacceptable, but unnecessary. All of this is so evident there ought to be no need even to discuss it. Effective life as a nation within a community of nations begins at the point when we ask ourselves, with a degree of urgency, what we are contributing, and potentially could, to the world beyond our borders, given that our own house is definitely going to be in order. Both tasks are no-one's business but our own.

Last of all, I want to return to my own particular community, my own neck of the woods. Creativity and creative criticism form the yeast which is essential to leavening every society. They provide its oxygen. Public support for the arts should make creative people into protagonists, rather than distrusting them or neutralising them. Those who take on the job of handing out the available money, however well-intentioned, will inevitably seek to impose their own agendas, which are animated by political and ethical views it is the business of creative people to dismantle, expose, ridicule and set in crisis. One single, monolithic government arts organisation cannot hope to foster the free play, the productive, at times apparently irresponsible chaos which allows a society to breathe and think. So the business in an independent Scotland of multifarious arts agencies, sometimes mutually oppositional in inspiration, would be to listen to and honour artists, rather than disciplining, regimenting or cowing them. It is perhaps inevitable that the arts administrator will be on a far higher salary than any of those involved in making art. But nobody should pretend that he, or she, knows better than the actual artist.

As I acknowledged, this is the group I belong to, the parish in which I worship. It is our business to make fun and provoke hilarity, but also to imagine and to teach, to offer a vision and an example. Several decades ago, writing from a seemingly hopeless predicament in communist Czechoslovakia, Václav Havel suggested that the real pay off from civic resistance, from creative networking in a society blighted by stagnation, comes while you are doing it. It consists of the relationships that emerge between individuals. It is such relationships that I would hope for in an independent Scotland, people empowered and using their power well, not acting submissively towards church or business or political authority (still so uniformly and depressingly male-dominated) but discovering an authority within themselves and responding, in surprising, even breath-taking ways, to its demands and promptings.

Vinska Gora, Slovenia, May 2012

NOTES ON CONTRIBUTORS

John Aberdein is a former herring fisherman, political activist and English teacher who grows tatties in Hoy and writes the odd novel. *Amande's Bed*, set in 1956 Aberdeen, scooped a Saltire First Book Award; *Strip the Willow*, centred in a contemporary Uberdeen, was named SAC Fiction of the Year, 2010.

Allan Armstrong is a retired teacher and former convenor of the Scottish Federation of Socialist Teachers. He was chair of the Lothians Anti-Poll Tax Federation. Allan is a Scottish internationalist, republican and communist and is on the Editorial Board of the magazine *Emancipation & Liberation* and the blog republicancommunist.org/blog.

Gordon Asher is an activist and cultural worker based in Glasgow. A member of the academic precariat, he works part-time at the University of the West of Scotland, the University of Strathclyde and the University of Glasgow – where he is also studying part-time for a PhD researching 'Learning and Education in Social Movements/Networks Working for Social Justice in Scotland'. Gordon is a co-editor of *Variant* – a multi-layered publishing project which brings creative practices and public discourse together.

Alan Bissett is a novelist, playwright and performer. He won the Glenfiddich Spirit of Scotland Writer of the Year 2011. His most recent novels, *Death of a Ladies' Man* and *Pack Men*, were shortlisted for the Scottish Mortgage Investment Trust Fiction of the Year awards in 2010 and 2012.

Jenni Calder has lived in Scotland since 1971, working as a free-lance writer and lecturer and from 1978 to 2001 at the National Museums of Scotland. She writes fiction and poetry as Jenni Daiches. Her new book *Lost in the Backwoods: Scots and the North American Wilderness* is due out in 2013.

Bob Cant is the editor of *Footsteps and Witnesses: Lesbian and Gay Lifestories from Scotland* (2008). He was a founder member of the Millthorpe Project which collects audio-lifestories of lesbian, gay, bisexual and transgender (LGBT) trade unionists. He has just completed his first novel.

Jo Clifford is a playwright and performer, many of whose 70+ plays have been performed internationally as well as in Scotland. She is currently turning her *Sex, Chips & The Holy Ghost* into a short film for Channel 4, making a book out of her *Gospel According to Jesus Queen of Heaven*, and completing a commission from the National Theatre of Scotland. Her *Great Expectations* will shortly open in the West End. She is the father of two amazing grown-up daughters, and is currently expecting her first grandchild.

Meaghan Delahunt was born in Melbourne and lives in Edinburgh. Her novels include *The Red Book*, *In the Blue House* – winner of the Saltire First Book Prize, a Scottish Arts Council Book of the Year prize and a Commonwealth Prize for Best First Book – and *To the Island*.

Douglas Dunn was born in Renfrewshire, and his collections of poetry include *Terry Street* (1969), *Elegies* (1985), *Northlight* (1988), *St Kilda's Parliament* (1991), and *New Selected Poems* (2003). He was a freelance writer for twenty years before being appointed Professor of English at St Andrews (1991-2008).

Margaret Elphinstone has published nine novels, including *The Sea Road, Hy Brasil, Voyageurs, Light* and *The Gathering Night*. She has lived and worked in various parts of Scotland including Shetland, Moray, Galloway, Edinburgh and Glasgow, and is an Emeritus Professor at the University of Strathclyde. She now lives in Galloway.

Leigh French is principal editor of *Variant* magazine: an intentionally free publication which brings creative practices and public discourse together, aiming to widen the involvement of a diverse readership in debate, discussion and awareness of the many interconnected cultural and social issues affecting society today.

Janice Galloway is the author of seven critically celebrated books. Her first novel, *The Trick is to Keep Breathing*, was published in 1990. Her latest book, *All Made Up*, is Scottish non-fiction Book of the Year for 2012. She has one husband and one son and likes living in Scotland.

Magi Gibson, poet and writer, was born and brought up in Kilsyth. She studied French and German at Glasgow University and now lives in Glasgow's West End with Irish comedy writer Ian Macpherson. In 2009 she became the first Makar of the City of Stirling in 500 years.

Alasdair Gray was born in Glasgow, 1934, graduated in Mural Design from Glasgow Art School in 1957 and has since lived by writing fiction which has been published in many other countries, by designing books (chiefly his own) and by painting.

Kirsty Gunn's latest work of fiction, *The Big Music*, set in the Highlands of Scotland, has just been published by Faber. She is Professor of Writing Practice and Study at the University of Dundee, a programme she created herself to be unlike all other traditional creative writing degrees, that is now in its fourth year.

Scott Hames (editor) lectures at the University of Stirling, and co-edits the *International Journal of Scottish Literature*. He has written widely on modern Scottish literature, especially James Kelman. The idea for this project is partly drawn from a forthcoming book on Scottish literary nationalism and the politics of 'voice'.

Kathleen Jamie was born in the west of Scotland in 1962. Her poetry collections to date include *The Overhaul* (Picador, 2012),

The Tree House (Picador 2004), which won both the Forward prize and the Scottish Book of the Year Award, *Jizzen* (Picador 1999) which won the Geoffrey Faber Memorial Award, and *Mr and Mrs Scotland are Dead*, shortlisted for the 2003 Griffin Prize. Kathleen also writes non-fiction including the highly regarded *Findings* and, more recently, *Sightlines*. She is Chair of Creative Writing at Stirling University, and lives with her family in Fife.

James Kelman was born in Glasgow, Scotland. His story collections include *Greyhound for Breakfast*, *The Good Times* and, most recently, *If it is your life*. His novel *How late it was, how late* won the 1994 Booker Prize; other novels include *Translated Accounts*, *You Have to be Careful in the Land of the Free* and *Kieron Smith, boy*. In 2009 and 2011 James Kelman was shortlisted for the Man Booker International Prize.

Tom Leonard's reprinted *outside the narrative* (poems 1965-2009) and the CD reading of his own and some Brecht poems are both available from Word Power Books. An anthology of personal political and critical prose 1973-2012 *Definite Articles* is due later in 2012. At his website www.tomleonard.co.uk an ongoing journal can be found.

Ken MacLeod has written thirteen novels, from *The Star Fraction* (1995) to *Intrusion* (2012). In 2009 he was Writer in Residence at the ESRC Genomics Policy and Research Forum. He is now Writer in Residence at the MA Creative Writing course, Edinburgh Napier University.

Aonghas MacNeacail, Borders-based, has been publishing poetry for nearly fifty years. Places he's read include Ireland, frequently (from Dublin to Tory Island), Tokyo, Seattle, the Finnish Arctic Circle, the UN Building in New York, and the Capitol in Rome. A Gaelic New and Selected, *Laughing at the Clock*, has just appeared from Polygon.

Kevin MacNeil is an award-winning poet, novelist, playwright and critic from the Outer Hebrides. He is also a keen cyclist and practitioner of Zen Buddhism. His books include *The Stornoway*

Way (Penguin), *A Method Actor's Guide to Jekyll and Hyde* (Polygon) and *Love and Zen in the Outer Hebrides* (Penguin). A Gaelic speaker with a degree in Ethnology, MacNeil has travelled extensively and is in favour of independence for Scotland.

Chad McCail (cover design) was born in 1961 in Manchester and grew up in Edinburgh. He lives and works in South Lanarkshire. Recently his interest in the way we bring up children has resulted in a large digital work showing a cutaway school, *Monoculture* (2010), and a puberty fairy tale, *Rites of Spring* (2011). www.chadmccail.co.uk

Denise Mina is the author of ten novels, three graphic novels, two plays and innumerable bits and bobs. She lives and works in Glasgow.

Don Paterson is the author of several collections of poetry, the most recent of which is *Rain*. He is Professor of Poetry at the University of St Andrews, and also works as an editor and musician.

James Robertson is a poet and novelist. His books include *The Testament of Gideon Mack*, *Joseph Knight* and *And the Land Lay Still*, which received the Saltire Society Book of the Year award in 2010.

Suhayl Saadi is a Glasgow-based novelist, playwright and radio writer described by the British Council as 'one of the most prolific and innovative British Asian writers of the past decade'. His novel *Psychoraag* was described by *The List* magazine/Scottish Book Trust as one of the hundred most important Scottish books of all time. His latest novel, *Joseph's Box*, was nominated for the IMPAC Prize 2011. www.suhaylsaadi.com.

Mike Small is an activist, writer and micro-publisher. He was a co-founder of *Product* magazine (first launched as *Red Herring* in 1998) as well as one of the group behind Indymedia Scotland. He has written for *Lobster* and *Variant* magazines and is currently a columnist for *The Guardian*. He is currently editor of *Bella*

Caledonia (bellacaledonia.org.uk) and contributed to *Despatches from the Invisible Revolution –New Public Thinking #1: Reflections on 2011* (ed. Dougald Hine & Keith Kahn-Harris).

Leela Sooben (typesetter) hails from Mauritius and has worked on several other Word Power Books publications, as well as other projects.

Gerda Stevenson – actor/writer/director; BAFTA Scotland Best Film Actress Award for *Blue Black Permanent*; twice nominated CATS awards; original plays and dramatisations of classic Scottish novels, BBC Radio 4; stage play *Federer Versus Murray* runner up for Best Scottish Contribution to Drama on Edinburgh Fringe, 2011; Associate Director Communicado Theatre Company; www.gerdastevenson.co.uk.

Christopher Whyte's fifth collection of Gaelic poems appeared in autumn 2012, with a book of 180 Tsvetaeva translations due out from Archipelago Press of New York in spring 2013. He taught from 1990 to 2005 in the Department of Scottish Literature at Glasgow University and now lives in Budapest, Hungary, where he writes full time.

Word Power Books (publisher) is an independent bookshop, publisher and distributor, based in Edinburgh. Our list of publications can be viewed online at www.word-power.co.uk.